Written upon the Heart

The Ten Commandments for Today's Christian

ANTHONY J. TOMASINO

WIPF & STOCK · Eugene, Oregon

Wipf and Stock Publishers
199 W 8th Ave, Suite 3
Eugene, OR 97401

Written upon the Heart
The Ten Commandments for Today's Christian
By Tomasino, Anthony J.
Copyright©2000 by Tomasino, Anthony J.
ISBN 13: 978-1-60608-181-5
Publication date 10/31/2008
Previously published by Kregel Publications, 2000

Contents

Introduction

In the spring of 1997, a debate that caught the attention of the entire nation raged in the U.S. House of Representatives. Lawmakers and concerned citizens on both sides of the issue argued that the very core values on which our society is based were at stake. It was a free speech issue. It was a church-state separation issue. It was a question of basic moral authority.

It was the issue of whether or not Alabama Circuit Court Judge Roy Moore would be allowed to display the Ten Commandments in his courtroom.

Judge Moore's attorneys argued in the media that there was far more at stake in this case than simply a matter of free expression. They argued that the Ten Commandments established the very principles on which our society—indeed, any just and fair society—must be founded. They implied that removing the Commandments from the courtroom would undermine the values that we hold dear. Perhaps such an action would even accelerate the downfall of America from its position of greatness in the world. They called on all Christian people everywhere to pray that the Ten Commandments would remain firmly affixed to the courtroom wall. But the arguments proved fruitless—the Supreme Court ruled that the Commandments had to go.

In June 1999, the Ten Commandments once again made the headlines. In response to a spate of violent incidents in high schools across the United States, the House of Representatives, seeming to thumb its collective nose at the Supreme Court, passed a bill giving states the right to display the Ten Commandments in public buildings. Again it was argued that the Commandments are the foundation for our morals and values. Perhaps if the Commandments were placed where our children would see them regularly, they would "sink in" and do what the parents were failing to do—provide some kind of moral compass for the confused youth.

Obviously, Americans are feeling that a crisis may be on the horizon. And the remedy, some seem to believe, could be as simple as giving our children two tablets of stone and checking the moral temperature again in the morning. The Ten Commandments are enjoying the limelight to an extent unparalled for centuries. Newspaper articles and editorials talk about their merits. Preachers and politicians prescribe them as a social panacea. A recent book on the Commandments, written by a popular radio psychologist, rocketed all the way to the top of the best-seller list, and perched there for several weeks. Our society is in search of answers—solid, no-nonsense answers. Many people who are sated with moral relativism are seeking an unambiguous code of conduct that could pull our country from the brink of the cesspool. And the Ten Commandments seem to embody the kind of rock-solid principles that could provide the firm place for us to plant our feet.

Now, as a pastor and student of the Scriptures, I'd be the last one to dampen enthusiasm for the Bible. Nonetheless, I do feel some words of caution are necessary here, for our society as a whole and Christians in particular. We need to bear in mind that the Ten Commandments possess no magical powers. Printing them on paper and pasting them to a wall won't create an impenetrable boundary that can banish the forces of darkness. Seeing the words on paper, or even committing them to memory, won't necessarily impel people to obey them. Our children could chant them every morning and evening and still grow up to be criminals. Knowing the Commandments is nothing. The Devil, I'm sure, knows them by heart.

Furthermore, the Ten Commandments aren't so unambiguous and unwavering as some seem to suppose. These short, pithy statements are open to a good deal of interpretation. Throughout the ages—beginning even in biblical times—scholars have argued over the meaning of certain words and phrases. The Commandments are so terse that even a single uncertain word can have big ramifications. We'll get into some of those issues later, as we discuss the different possible translations of the various commands.

And ambiguity isn't the only problem with the Commandments. Jesus himself taught that obeying the Ten Commandments alone isn't enough to fulfill one's religious and moral duty. Jesus supplemented them, and even superseded them, with his own instructions. As Christians, when Jesus talks, we need to listen. If he regarded the Commandments to be an insufficient guide for Christian morality, perhaps we should reconsider society's renewed "zeal" for them, also.

And finally, the Ten Commandments were never designed to be a general rule for morality. They aren't meant to be the foundation of law for any decent society. The Commandments were designed for a specific people—the people who lived in a covenant relationship with God. They were written to operate in a specific context—the context of God's relationship with his chosen people. And in spite of some people's ideas to the contrary, the citizenry of the United States of America is not God's chosen people. The Ten Commandments are not designed to be the rule of conduct for American society and justice.

Now having said that much, someone might just be wondering, "Then why study the Ten Commandments at all?" That's a fair question. And the answer is readily at hand for believers. The Ten Commandments weren't written for our modern American society; they were written for the people of God. And that's who we are, we who believe in Jesus Christ and live in relationship with God through Christ. If the Ten Commandments have relevance for anyone today, it'll be for us.

But the Ten Commandments aren't transparent and unambiguous. The deceptively simple words are packed with meaning and must be understood in their historical and literary contexts. That requires that we do some study. Jesus cut to the heart of the Commandments; he expounded on them; he challenged his disciples to look beyond the surface of the words to the intention of the Author. And if the

Commandments are going to have real significance in our Christian lives, we have to do the same thing.

And finally, the Commandments aren't magic. They'll do nothing for us if we just read them or even commit them to memory. We have to apply them to our lives and our situations. We must live by them, allowing them to guide us each step along our way. And that can take some reflection on our part, some mulling over of the implications of these ancient words. Some hypothetical situations and examples from real life will help, as well.

In this brief study, we won't be looking at the Ten Commandments as a general moral code or a collection of wise rules for society. We'll be considering the Commandments as God's instructions for his chosen people. Of course, there'll be implications for our society, as well. After all, we Christians are members of our societies, and we can play a powerful role in shaping societal values and transforming institutions. But we won't make a difference by quoting the Ten Commandments to our neighbor. We can only make a difference by embodying the Commandments and living them out in our relationships with God and our fellow human beings.

o n e

The Christian and the Law

IT WAS AN EVENT THAT threatened to disrupt our community life. It occurred during the mid-eighties, when I was a student at Asbury Theological Seminary in Wilmore, Kentucky. On Lexington Avenue, at the crossroads just north of the Asbury College and Asbury Seminary campuses, a small convenience store opened for business. The store sold no alcoholic beverages, Wilmore being a dry town by community decree. Nor were there any adult magazines or lottery tickets sold behind the counter. But the little store's owners had thumbed their noses at local custom by opening their doors for business on Sunday afternoons—the only store in the whole town that dared to do so.

The faculty of Asbury College was angered by the audacity of the store's owners. The college president made an impassioned speech to the Asbury College community, describing how this event could lead to the moral decay of the entire town. Traditional values were being undermined, and this incident was only the beginning. Preachers and professors expressed their concerns for the souls of the student body. Many of them believed it was a violation of the Ten Commandments to make purchases on Sunday. Others were worried that college and seminary students would end up working on Sunday afternoons, instead of sanctifying the day for worship and rest. Soon, they predicted, other businesses in town would feel that they, too, must remain open on Sundays in order to compete. The stores might even extend their hours to Sunday mornings, forcing students to miss Sunday morning worship.

The solution, according to the college president and some faculty, was a strict boycott of the little store. Letters should be written to its owners demanding that they cease the secular practice of Sunday sales. If necessary, the college community would go before the city council and seek an order banning Sunday commerce in Wilmore.

Meanwhile, on the other side of Lexington Avenue, the Asbury Seminary community barely seemed touched by all the uproar. Of course we talked about it, and some students and faculty expressed genuine concern that the sanctity of the town was under assault. Many in the seminary community, however, had made an occasional Sunday drive to nearby Nicholasville for a gallon of milk, some diapers, or a package of toilet tissue. Wouldn't it be convenient—and, in fact, a *better* observance of the Sabbath—to have a store a mere two blocks away, so they could get their milk and be back home resting within in a few minutes instead of a half an hour? A number of students openly expressed support for the store, while many more, I believe, secretly patronized the establishment.

When I graduated from seminary and left Wilmore behind, the controversy was still simmering. But I had reason to suspect that the boycott would fail. One Sunday afternoon, as I had dashed into the store to pick up a loaf of bread, I bumped into a high-ranking member of the Asbury Seminary faculty.

On one side of Lexington Avenue—Asbury College—some people held strong opinions both on the importance of keeping Sunday as a holy Sabbath and on how the Sabbath should be observed. On the other side of the street—Asbury Seminary—the issue seemed far less significant. Few of the students or faculty really seemed concerned about the impact that Sunday commerce would have on Wilmore. It was quite a joke among the students who'd attended both schools. Typically, attitudes toward obeying the "Law" were far more relaxed at the seminary than they were at the college. Students said that on the west side of Lexington Avenue they lived under law, while on the east they lived under grace.

Law and grace. Are the two concepts incompatible? When we think of law, we often think of burdensome rules and regulations, of fear and punishment. Grace, on the other hand, conjures up images of freedom and acceptance, of love and mercy. Law, we sometimes hear, is characteristic of the old covenant between God and Israel. It regulated the way that the nation of Israel related to her God. The old covenant was, of course, a dismal failure, since Israel could never keep the Law. Indeed, the nation was eventually destroyed because of her failure. We of the church, however, are under the new covenant between God and humanity. The Law, some say, has been rendered obsolete by the work of Jesus Christ. The new covenant between God and the church is marked by unconditional acceptance of the sinner who turns to Christ in faith. And so, say some Christians, the Law is as outmoded as the Edsel.

It sounds like a good assessment. It even sounds biblical. But was the Law really a failure? And is it really obsolete?

If we're going to give the Law a fair trial, it's necessary to understand the nature and function of the Law. Why did God give the Israelites a set of rules to govern their daily affairs? Were the Israelites really expected to keep the Ten Commandments and the other biblical law codes? Only after considering such questions as these can we determine whether the Law has any relevance in the Christian life.

THE PURPOSE OF THE LAW

As long as there have been human beings living together for their mutual benefit—a relationship that we call "society"—there's been a need for laws. Laws existed long before there was even a means of writing them down. Ancient tribal societies followed law codes that were passed on orally from generation to generation. To the members of the tribe, these laws were powerfully binding. They gave tribe members a sense of identity and security. Each tribe had its own laws, enforced by the tribal chief or elders.

Then, kingdoms were set up in the world, incorporating people from different tribes. In order to bring some unity to the kingdoms, the ancient kings had to assert authority over the tribal chieftains—and the tribal laws. So about twenty-one hundred years before the time of Christ, a Sumerian king named Ur-Nammu (of the city-state of Ur) recorded a written law code. In part, its purpose was to provide guidelines to judges for properly deciding the cases brought before them. But the law code was also designed to demonstrate Ur-Nammu's authority over the diverse peoples in his kingdom. His laws were engraved on pillars erected around the borders of Sumerian territory so those entering his land would know they were now subject to the laws of the king of Ur.

The most famous ancient law code outside the Old Testament came from the Babylonian king Hammurabi. Hammurabi, who died around 1750 B.C., is famous for producing a law code that's similar in several ways to the Law of Moses. Like Ur-Nammu, Hammurabi engraved his laws on pillars and displayed them around the borders of Babylon. At the top of the pillars, Hammurabi is depicted receiving the laws from the hand of Shamash, the Babylonian god of justice. Hammurabi claimed that his law code derived not from a king, but from the gods. The king was merely responsible for carrying out the divine will. As with Ur-Nammu, Hammurabi's public posting of the laws around the borders of his land served to demonstrate his authority over any other law—including old tribal code—that might be observed in his kingdom. It's interesting, however, that court records unearthed in Babylon reveal that Hammurabi's Law Code was seldom consulted by the judges. Their decisions rarely bore any resemblance to what Hammurabi prescribed.

So law codes in the ancient Near East were not, in effect, binding regulations that dictated how decisions should be made in the courts. Rather, they were one way that the king attempted to demonstrate his sovereignty over his subjects. The ancient kings imposed the law because they had the *right* to do so.

But how does the function of law in ancient Sumer and Babylon compare to the role of the Law in ancient Israel? In some ways, it's very similar. When the Israelites were slaves in Egypt, they didn't live without laws. They were subject to the laws of Egypt. Furthermore, the Israelite people probably followed ancient tribal customs that governed their relations with one another and with their God. So God didn't give Israel the Ten Commandments because they had no laws.

He, in part, gave them the Law to *demonstrate his sovereignty* over his people—the people he'd personally created and redeemed.

At the very beginning of the biblical laws, God declares his right to an influential role in Israelite life. The Ten Commandments begin with the powerful declaration, "I am the LORD your God, who brought you out of Egypt, out of the land of slavery" (Exod. 20:2). Not only had the Lord created the Israelite nation at the call of Abraham (Gen. 12:1-3), he demonstrated his continuing care by redeeming them, "buying them back" from Egyptian slavery. Thus, God established his right to be Israel's Lawgiver. No other gods, no other spirits, had created Israel or delivered them from slavery. The Lord's relationship with Israel was unique and exclusive.

This unique relationship is the rationale behind the biblical laws: The laws weren't designed so much to make Israel better than other people, but to make Israel different from other people. In Leviticus 11:44-45 and 20:7, for instance, God tells the Israelites that they are to make themselves holy by keeping the laws. Holiness doesn't mean that all the Israelites were expected to be perfect, saintly creatures without moral flaws. In fact, the Hebrew word "holy," *qadosh,* doesn't have anything to do with a person's moral condition—at least not directly. Rather, the word "holy" simply means "set apart for God." It's a word that could be used to describe the altar in the sanctuary (Exod. 30:10), the Sabbath day (20:8), the dirt on Mount Sinai (3:5), or anything else that's set apart for God's use.

So, when the Bible says that keeping the Law makes the Israelites holy, it means that the Law distinguished Israel from the other peoples of the world. The Israelites were God's unique possession: "You are to be holy to me because I, the LORD, am holy, and I have set you apart from the nations to be my own" (Lev. 20:26). So the laws were not specifically designed to make Israel more moral. What, for instance, do the Jewish dietary laws have to do with being moral? There's nothing intrinsically moral or righteous in passing up the ham at a wedding reception or refusing to indulge in a shrimp cocktail. On the other hand, doing so does distinguish one from the other guests at the party.

Like the ancient kings of Babylon, God gave Israel the laws partly to demonstrate his kingly authority over his people. And also, like the ancient Babylonian magistrates, God was often quite lenient in enforcing those laws. For example, the Law clearly states that an adulterer was to be stoned to death (Lev. 20:10), yet God allowed David and Bathsheba to live after they'd committed adultery with each other (2 Sam. 11–12). He even commanded the prophet Hosea to marry an adulteress rather than have her stoned (Hos. 3:1). The written law codes, it seems, were designed to serve more as models than binding obligations.

That doesn't mean that God didn't take the Law seriously. It simply demonstrates that, even in the Old Testament, grace is present. Mercy wasn't an invention of the New Testament writers.

Positions on Christian Responsibility

The biblical Law, then, distinguished Israel as God's unique possession. But is the Law irrelevant for the Christian? Can we ignore the Law because we aren't Israelites in the physical sense? Or do we—as the spiritual descendants of Israel, God's new "holy nation"—have a responsibility to keep the Law in the same manner that ancient Israel did?

Opinions on the matter differ widely. Some Christians regard keeping the Law as their holy obligation, essential for the salvation of their souls. Didn't Jesus say that he hadn't come to destroy the Law but to fulfill it, and that anyone who disregarded the Law would be considered the least in the kingdom of heaven (Matt. 5:17–19)? Christians who hold this opinion are often considered "legalistic." Although many of them would strongly affirm that they are saved by God's grace through faith in Christ, they also would argue that the gift of salvation brings certain responsibilities for proper conduct. If you ignore the Law, you do so at the peril of your eternal soul.

This position has the merit of making one's responsibility to God unambiguous. You don't have to wonder if you're behaving the way that God wants you to; there are written requirements for your behavior. People who hold this position, however, sometimes lay a difficult burden on themselves—a burden too heavy for a human being to bear. A few years ago, a friend of mine was distressed when a member of her church had committed suicide. "Tony, he was one of the strongest Christians I ever knew," she said. "He taught our young adult Sunday school class, and he'd take the teenagers to the mall on Saturday to witness to people. He didn't drink, he didn't swear. He wouldn't even go to a dance—unless he was going to get someone saved. How could someone so devoted to God ever kill himself?" I couldn't know, of course, what had been going on in the young man's mind. But I suspect that he believed that God expected him to maintain impossibly high standards of conduct. This young man imposed such a heavy burden on himself—a burden that God never required—that he finally could bear it no longer. I hope that God has granted him a peace in heaven that he couldn't find in this world.

Another position on the Law maintains that it represents the perfect model for Christian life. According to people who hold this position, keeping the Law isn't essential for salvation, but it makes good sense. God had important reasons for giving the Law, they argue, and we'd do well not to ignore its precepts (cf. Rom. 7:7–12). Christians holding this position sometimes try to demonstrate that various laws weren't just given on a whim. Rather, they claim keeping the Law brings tangible benefits to our spirits, minds, and bodies. They might argue, for instance, that keeping the Sabbath gives our bodies a much-needed chance to recharge, or that the kosher (dietary) laws show us the most healthful way to eat. People who hold this position argue that the reason Jews were forbidden to eat pork is because the flesh of swine wasn't good for people living in the Near Eastern climate.

There's nothing new in this way of looking at the Law. In fact, in the book of Deuteronomy, Moses recounts before the Israelites the benefits of keeping God's Law: the people would multiply; their fields and flocks would be fertile; they would suffer no illness; their enemies would flee before them, etc. (Deut. 7:12–16; 11:13–23). In Daniel 1, the kosher laws are put to the test in order to demonstrate their benefits. According to the story, the Jewish youths Daniel, Shadrach, Meshach, and Abednego, who were among those chosen to be trained for service to the Babylonian king, refused to eat the king's food. Instead, they continued to follow their own diet. After only a week, they appeared healthier than all the other young men in the king's training program.

Outside of the Bible, too, Jewish teachers argued the healthful benefits of observing the Law. The Jewish philosopher Philo of Alexandria (born ca. 40 B.C.) asserted that the biblical laws reflected the laws of nature and so represented the "natural" way to a good life. The historian Josephus (born ca. A.D. 40) defended at some length the reasonable and beneficial nature of the laws in that they caused the Jewish nation to be perceived as the most civilized of people. So, even if keeping the Law weren't an obligation, it would still be a good idea. And such is the opinion of some Christians, as well.

Still other Christians regard the observance of Old Testament Law to be legalism, slavery, even apostasy. We have been freed by Christ, they argue. Why would we want to entangle ourselves with a yoke of bondage that was intended for another time and people (Gal. 5:1)? If we insist on trying to live by the standards of the Old Testament, we make Christ's sacrifice for us null and void. In its most extreme form, this view leads to a total disregard of any moral standards. Such a belief is called "antinomianism" ("against the law") and has been condemned as a heresy by the church. But, regarding the Old Testament Law as obsolete doesn't necessarily lead a Christian into immorality. If believers allow the Holy Spirit to guide their behaviors by the standards encouraged by the New Testament, they can still live a life pleasing to God, even without the Law.

New Testament Controversy

None of these positions is necessarily the most virtuous. Sincere, obedient Christians are found in all three camps. The debate isn't so much one of heretics against orthodox believers but of true disciples seeking to understand God's will for their lives. Even in the days of the apostles Christians debated the significance of the Law. Jesus and the first disciples were, of course, Jewish, so they naturally obeyed the Old Testament laws. But as the church expanded beyond the borders of Judea, it took in many converts who were not Jewish. The question was inevitable: Were these new Christians required to follow the Jewish traditions? In the church located in Galatia, a region of what is now Turkey, some taught that non-Jews who wished to become Christians were first required to become Jewish converts. These teachers—sometimes called "Judaizers"—proclaimed that every Christian was obligated to keep the Old Testament laws in such matters as circumcision, keeping kosher, and observing the Sabbath. But across the sea in Greece, the Corinthians had a different idea: there, the motto of the day was "All things are lawful to me!" In other words, the Corinthians didn't believe they were required to keep *any* of the Old Testament laws. All Christians were free to follow the dictates of conscience in all matters. And in ancient Greece, the conscience of even a Christian could allow quite a bit of leeway!

Because of such diverse opinions, the church leaders felt compelled to formulate an official position. And so, as recorded in Acts 15, the first church council was convened in Jerusalem sometime around A.D. 49 or 50, to discuss the matter of Christians and the Law. The great leaders of the church were in attendance: Peter and John, James, Paul and Barnabas, along with a great assembly of believers. Their stated purpose was to consider the insistent claim of certain teachers (former members of the Jewish Pharisee sect) that the new Gentile (i.e., non-Jewish) Christians had to be circumcised and had to obey the Law of Moses.

Peter, the untrained fisherman, argued eloquently in opposition to the Pharisaic position. He related how he'd been directed by God to bring the gospel to the Gentiles, and many of them had accepted his teachings. As a seal on their belief, God had given them the gift of the Holy Spirit, just as the Spirit had been given to the Jews. To Peter, this gift demonstrated that God had accepted the Gentiles just as they were, uncircumcised and "unkosher." "Why would you put on the Gentiles a yoke that neither we nor our fathers could bear?" he asked. "We believe that we are saved by the grace of Jesus Christ, just as they are" (cf. Acts 15:10–11). Paul and Barnabas, too, related wonderful stories of God's miraculous works among the Gentiles. In the light of such evidence, the church leadership was compelled to accept the Gentile converts just as they were—just as God had already accepted them.

The Gentiles were not, however, given *carte blanche*—allowed to behave any way they saw fit. The apostles and elders drafted a letter that contained an outline of what were regarded as Christian essentials (Acts 15:23–29). They finished with these words:

> It seemed good to the Holy Spirit and to us not to burden you with anything beyond the following requirements: You are to abstain from food sacrificed to idols, from blood, from the meat of strangled animals and from sexual immorality. You will do well to avoid these things. (vv. 28–29)

At first reading, these instructions seem a little strange. The apostles appear to have overlooked some really important matters. They said nothing, for instance, about murder, or stealing, or lying. Would the church fathers have forbidden the Gentile believers to indulge in pornography but allow them to commit murder? Were Gentiles allowed to steal or slander but prohibited from eating a steak medium rare? It's obvious that these instructions were *not* intended to serve as a full exposition on Christian morality. Rather, only some specific laws were in dispute at this time—laws dealing with practices that were peculiar to the Jews.

The first three regulations given here—abstaining from food sacrificed to idols, from blood, and from the meat of strangled animals—all have to do with what one may or may not eat. They address the issue of whether or not Gentiles were required to keep kosher. Could non-Jewish Christians eat pork? Could they eat lobster? Did they have to learn all the various laws that the Pharisees had devised for a proper Jewish diet? The Jerusalem Council answered no, as long as Christians observed certain basic regulations of diet. First, they weren't to eat food sacrificed to idols. In those days, meat from sacrificial animals was sold in temple restaurants as a source of revenue. Purchasing such meat would mean that one was patronizing the pagan temple. Furthermore, since idol worship often involved "sharing a meal" with the idol, non-Christians or naive believers could get the impression that Christians who dined at the pagan temple restaurant were endorsing idolatry (see 1 Cor. 8:1–13).

The next prohibition enjoined the Christians not to eat blood. This commandment, mentioned several times in the Law of Moses (e.g., Lev. 17:10–14), actually went back before Moses to the time of

Noah. After Noah and his family emerged from the ark, God gave human beings permission to eat any animals on earth. But he strictly commanded Noah that he was not to eat the blood, because the blood represented the very life force of the creature (Gen. 9:4–5). In pagan religions, it was common for people to drink the blood of animals in order to obtain supernatural power, or blood might be poured into a tomb in order to "feed" the spirits of the dead. The Bible strongly condemns such practices and the pagan beliefs behind them. The life force represented by the blood was supposed to return to God alone. No human being was allowed to consume it.

The Council decision regarding strangled animals—considered a delicacy in the ancient world—goes back to the same principle. The meat of animals slaughtered in this fashion was still infused with blood. The blood wasn't allowed to drain away, as it was when the animals were slaughtered with a knife. Such meat was thus taboo to Christians.

The final guideline that the Jerusalem Council issued, abstaining from sexual immorality, doesn't seem on the surface to have been addressing a matter of Jewish ritual. But in fact, this ruling might well have been designed to address the question of Gentile circumcision. In Jewish traditions of the day, circumcision was viewed as a hygienic practice, one that removed impurity from the body (note Isaiah 52:1, where the words "uncircumcised" and "defiled" are used as synonyms). And among Jews in Jesus' day, cleanliness was a very important concept (see Mark 7:1–23). The Talmud contained literally hundreds of teachings concerning the proper way to wash. By demanding that the Gentiles be circumcised, the Pharisaic teachers in the church were trying to impose their own standards of hygiene on the Gentile Christians. Because they weren't circumcised, the teachers argued, the Gentiles were defiled, unclean. But the Jerusalem Council replied that such a procedure was unnecessary; in order to be spiritually clean, the Gentiles merely had to abstain from sexual immorality.

THE PRINCIPLE BEHIND THE DECISION

This earliest church ruling by the Jerusalem Council on Christians and the Law didn't resolve the theoretical issue of whether or not

Gentile Christians were obligated to keep all the Old Testament laws. Rather, the Council merely issued a ruling concerning the observance of certain specific laws. The Gentiles (much to their relief, I'm sure) were exempted from keeping the laws related specifically to Israelite behavior, like circumcision and keeping kosher.

So the Jerusalem Council had made a distinction that isn't clear in the Old Testament itself. They assumed there were certain laws that govern moral behavior, and other laws that specifically govern the unique practices of the Israelites. It was a helpful, and necessary, distinction. But what did the Council decision say about the moral part of the law? Were the Gentiles—and all Christians, for that matter—still under obligation to keep the moral laws?

The answer is clearly no—if "under obligation" means required for the salvation of their souls. Peter stated before the Jerusalem Council that all Christians are saved as a free gift of God's grace, not through doing good deeds. Keeping laws—whether that law consists of many rules or only a few—can never justify us before God. We all stand in need of God's mercy. This being the case, the instructions that the church leaders gave to the new Christians— abstaining from food sacrificed to idols, from blood, and from sexual immorality—couldn't have been anything more than guidelines. They weren't requirements for entrance into heaven. Nobody was compelled to obey them, except by his or her love for God and a desire to be pleasing to him. As the Jerusalem Council wrote to the Gentiles, we "do well" to obey these rules, but we won't save ourselves through any such observance.

So, in what sense are these guidelines "requirements"? I think of them as essential in the same way that maintaining my car is essential. My car would run if all I ever did was put gas in the tank. If I never washed it, never rotated the tires, never changed the wiper blades, my car would still run. But how long would it keep running? And how well would it run? After thirty or forty thousand miles, my car would be a menace on the road, a danger to myself and everyone around me. Of course, my owner's manual says that I *must* change the oil every three thousand miles. It's worded as a requirement, but nobody's going to show up at my door and force me to do it. There's no law demanding I follow the maintenance schedule. But if I want my car to operate properly, certain tasks are essential.

In a similar sense, we Christians are under obligation—not to keep the Old Testament Law, but to keep a moral directive called the "law of the Spirit." Paul speaks about this law in his letter to the church at Rome. In Romans 7-8, Paul writes about his struggle to obey the Old Testament Law and traditions, and his repeated failures to do so. His spirit was willing, but his flesh was weak. And so, over and over again, he found himself unable to do what the Law says he should do and unable to be righteous according to the standards of the Law. Thus, he stood under the condemnation of the Law unable, in spite of all his efforts, to save himself (7:7-25). But the law of the Spirit, he proclaims, frees us from this bondage to sin and death. It allows us to fulfill the requirements of the Law in our bodies, because the Spirit of God empowers us to choose not to sin (8:1-4). For this reason, he continues, we're obligated to live righteous lives, not because it will save us and not because the Law requires us to do so, but simply because the Spirit of God empowers us to do so (8:12). There's no excuse for a life of sinful habits.

The final chapter of this book considers how the Spirit can empower us to fulfill the requirements of the Law. For now, suffice it to say that Christians aren't free from the burden of the Law so we can live lives of lawlessness. Rather, we're free from an external set of rules so that we can give obedience to an internal law—the law of the Spirit.

THE IMPORTANCE OF THE LAW

According to the New Testament, keeping the Law cannot save us. Salvation is a free gift, given to anyone who turns to Christ in faith. Yet, we don't have license to live however we may choose, as if no authority exists external to ourselves. The models for our behavior are established, in part, by the teachings of the Old Testament.

Paul states explicitly that the Law is still important for the Christian. The Law, he writes, is good and holy (Rom. 7:12), since it teaches us the nature of sin (Rom. 4:20; 7:7). In his letter to the Galatians, Paul describes the Law using the idea of the pedagogue

(Gal. 3:24–25). Strictly speaking, the pedagogue was a slave who was responsible for taking the children to school, keeping them in line during their lessons, and then bringing them home again. In more general usage, the term could be used for any tutor. The Law, Paul writes, was a tutor. Before Jesus came, the Law kept Israel in check, like the slave who leads the children to class. Through the Law, the Jewish people were instructed about God's nature and love. The Law's simple guidelines taught the meaning of sin and righteousness. But with the coming of Christ, believers reached maturity. They're no longer children under the authority of the tutor.

Many Christians have found that the Law can work as a tutor in their own journey to faith. But in striving to live according to a set of rules and regulations, they've become frustrated (like the suicide victim I wrote about earlier). At the point of their frustration, they can, like Paul, give up their striving to win God's approval. They then come to realize that salvation is God's free gift. The great evangelist John Wesley, founder of the Methodist movement, faced just such a crisis in his own life. He was an Anglican priest who had always aspired to serve God with all his being. And yet, in spite of all his striving to please God, Wesley felt empty and afraid. On a missionary trip to America, the ship in which Wesley traveled was caught in a storm. He became terrified that he would die and that his soul would be lost forever. Wesley's life was spared, and he then searched in earnest for a faith that could give him confidence in his salvation. It wasn't until he learned to trust in Christ alone for his salvation, not depending on his own efforts, that he became fully empowered to do the work to which God had called him. His struggles to obtain righteousness through the law led him to a true appreciation of salvation by grace.

The Law does not, however, lose its value for us as soon as we're saved. Using the analogy of the tutor, when people graduate from school, they shouldn't try to forget everything they've learned. Even though we're not under the authority of the tutor, the lessons remain with us. Likewise, while the Law no longer has binding authority over us, its teachings remain "a lamp to [our] feet and a light for [our] path" (Ps. 119:105). It provides standards for our Christian conduct.

Paul emphasized this very point with the Corinthians. As mentioned above, at Corinth the catchphrase was "All things are lawful to me," or "I can do anything I want." But Paul replies that while we're not bound to the Law, neither should we ignore it.

> Do you not know that the wicked will not inherit the kingdom of God? Do not be deceived: Neither the sexually immoral nor idolaters nor adulterers nor male prostitutes nor homosexual offenders nor thieves nor the greedy nor drunkards nor slanderers nor swindlers will inherit the kingdom of God. (1 Cor. 6:9–10)

All things may indeed be "lawful" for the Christian, but not all things are profitable. All things are lawful, but not all things will aid us in our growth toward godliness. And those who habitually break the precepts of the Law, says Paul, have no place in the kingdom of God.

Furthermore, Paul writes, while we may be free to do whatever we want, we must consider that some behaviors might cause others to stumble in their Christian walk (10:23–33). Paul uses the example of eating food that had been sacrificed to idols. We know that idols are nothing but statues, he says, and that food is food. But if eating meat from idol worship offends somebody or gives someone the wrong impression, it's best not to partake. We're not under a law, he writes, but we must not be responsible for the downfall of a weaker brother or sister.

You could say that Paul had to "lay down the Law" for the Corinthians because they acted irresponsibly with their Christian freedom. Too much freedom for an undisciplined mind can be intoxicating—and deadly. When my son Vincent was two years old, he had to obey many rules that were beyond his comprehension. He wasn't allowed, for example, to play around the stove when Daddy or Mommy was cooking. He wasn't old enough to understand that the stove gets hot and that he could be seriously injured. But when he got a little older and he'd been splattered by flying grease a few times, he learned that the hot stove was better avoided. The law wasn't necessary any more. But until Vincent understood the principle, he needed the rule.

The same is often true in our Christian growth. Until we learn to act out of principle, we need rules. Several years ago, I was involved with a denomination that prohibits its members from drinking alcohol. Some of the ministers and denominational leaders, however, felt the time had come for the ban to be lifted. Most modern Western Christians, reasoned the leaders, would act responsibly with regard to alcohol consumption, and imposing a rule governing such behavior seemed rather legalistic. But the bishop from Africa said he would oppose any move to "repeal Prohibition" in his denomination. "My people are not ready yet for such freedom," he said. "They still need explicit guidance for their behavior." So the move to eliminate the law didn't come to a vote. Until a Christian has matured to the point of internalizing principles of the faith, he or she may need the discipline of a rule.

PRINCIPLE-LY PERFECT

Jesus bears strong witness to the role of the Law in providing discipline. In his teaching, he made constant reference to the Law, holding it up as the *minimum* standard for Christian righteousness. In the Sermon on the Mount, Jesus taught that unless we fulfill the Law and surpass its requirements, we aren't truly fit for the kingdom of heaven (Matt. 5:17-20). The Ten Commandments say we're not supposed to murder, but Jesus says we shouldn't even bear malice against another (vv. 21-22). The Commandments say we shouldn't commit adultery, but Jesus says we shouldn't even harbor lust in our hearts (vv. 27-28). In his teaching on divorce, too, Jesus held that the legal code, which allowed divorce in many cases, was really only the minimum standard— a concession to our sinful natures. God's desire for us is that our marriages last a lifetime (19:1-9). So the Law provided the standard, but true righteousness goes beyond the Law to an internalization of the principles behind the laws. Knowing the Law can keep us from doing the wrong thing. Living by the principles behind the laws impels us to do the right thing. Jesus goes so far as to say that by keeping such principles, we will be perfect, as our Father in heaven is perfect (5:48).

Perfection—what a daunting prospect! Could Jesus seriously expect us to be perfect? Doesn't the popular bumper sticker say, "Christians aren't perfect—just forgiven"? A best-selling author recently argued that Jesus never expected that we'd be able to keep the principles expressed in the Sermon on the Mount. Instead, writes the author, Jesus was showing us how impossible it is to please God and how much we need grace. God's standard is perfection, and of course we can never be perfect. And yet, as consoling as that sounds, it's not scriptural—if we mean "perfect" according to the Bible's use of the word "perfect."

The Greek word for "perfect," *teleios,* doesn't imply that we never make mistakes. Rather, this kind of "perfection" denotes something that's carried out to its proper end—for example, a task brought to completion, or an animal that's grown to maturity, or a tally of grain that fills up its full measure. So when Jesus commands us to aspire to perfection, he's telling us to "fill up" our righteousness; not to do the minimum required, but to carry out the Law's original intention. We're to aspire to perfection that's based on principles that we internalize, rather than external precepts that we feel compelled to obey. In this way, we *can* be perfect, as God is perfect. God's righteousness doesn't occur because he obeys the rules. It's his very nature to be righteous. Our righteousness, too, shouldn't be based on compulsion or rules. Rather, our righteousness should arise naturally from a godly character. So our perfection isn't dependent on our proper adherence to rules and regulations—it needs internal, motivating principles.

If we're to be perfect Christians, then, it's important that we understand the principles behind the Law. Through these principles, we learn God's intention for humanity—not to be bound by fear and condemnation, but to be released for joyous growth in grace. And the best place to discern these principles is in the foundation of the entire Old Testament law code—the Ten Commandments.

QUESTIONS FOR REFLECTION

1. What does "holiness" mean to you? Do you ever think of yourself as holy?
2. How does law function in our society today? Compare and contrast our laws with the laws of the ancient Israelites.

3. Do you ever do things that are illegal? How might you justify breaking the law?

4. If everyone were a dedicated Christian, would we still need laws?

5. In what areas of your life do you still need the discipline of rules? In what areas do you live by principle alone?

t w o

What Are the Ten Commandments?

Then God spoke all these words, saying . . .
—Exodus 20:1 NASB

IN JEWISH TRADITION, no figure looms so mighty as that of Moses. To him, the rabbis ascribed all the laws of Israel—not merely the written laws, but all the oral traditions recorded in the rabbinic holy books, as well. These oral traditions, they claimed, were passed on by word of mouth from Moses throughout the generations, until they were finally collected and written down by the rabbis (from reluctant necessity). To the Jews, Moses has long been synonymous with the Law.

Jesus also speaks of Moses as the giver of the Law (John 7:19). Indeed, throughout the New Testament, the name "Moses" can almost be regarded as shorthand for "the Law" (Mark 1:44; Acts 21:21; 2 Cor. 3:15). When Jesus was transfigured before his disciples, the figure of Moses appeared and stood beside him, along with the figure of Elijah. Moses appears as the representative of the Law, while Elijah appears to represent the prophets. Jesus, of course, revealed in his glory, is superior to both of them.

To Jews and Christians alike, Moses' reception of the Law on Mount Sinai was the defining event of Moses' life. He's come to be known as the Great Lawgiver. But technically speaking, Moses wasn't *literally* the lawgiver. According to the Bible, he was the Law *receiver*. The Law was given by none other than God himself. The authority of the Law didn't derive from Moses' personal power or special office. The authority of the Law came from God, who not only authored it but also would oversee its execution.

Some cynics have argued that the biblical author might have been "peeking" at Hammurabi's Code when he wrote that God gave the Law to Moses. The Babylonian king, Hammurabi, made a similar claim about his own law, that it had been given to him by Shamash, the Babylonian god of justice. And in fact, almost every ancient law code begins with the same assertion: the law didn't come from the king, it came from heaven. To the cynic, that means that the kings were simply trying to scare their subjects into submission to the law: "Better be good, or the god will get you!"

A better explanation exists, however, for the similar claims of divine inspiration that were made about ancient law codes. These codes demonstrate a bit of common human wisdom that many modern people have forgotten—we human beings need authority external to ourselves. In order for the Law to stand over us, it must in some sense be above us. Its authority can't simply be based on the general consensus of human society at some given time in history, or the law has no firm basis. It wouldn't have the power to oversee us. Instead, the law would be our slave, subject to our collective whims, fads, and fashions. Ancient nations, even the pagan ones, had the insight and humility to recognize the need for an external, ultimate authority. Modern people are generally more shortsighted and self-assured.

But the inspiration that the ancient pagan law codes attempted to claim are dim reflections of the high truth that we see in the Bible. What pagan cultures conveyed through assertions or through myths, the Bible conveys through the historical account of Moses on Mount Sinai. The Law is the gift of God, and Moses was merely the delivery man.

THE FORMS OF ANCIENT LAW

The ancient law codes and the biblical law code share the assertion that they're divinely inspired. But the similarities don't end there. The biblical and nonbiblical laws also share some common *forms.* When the laws of the ancient kingdoms were written down, and even when they were still passed on by oral tradition, they followed a pattern. We can distinguish that pattern throughout all the law codes of the ancient Near East and through the Bible, as well.

Take, for example, the most famous of the ancient law codes, the Code of Hammurabi. It was established by the great king of ancient Akkad (Babylon) around 1750 B.C.—at least three hundred years before the time of Moses. The 282 sections of this code cover such topics as theft, commerce, marriage, adoption, rates and wages, and the treatment of slaves. And the laws follow a very simple pattern. They begin with a description of the circumstances: "If a citizen has accused and charged another citizen of murder, but he hasn't proven the charge . . ." This initial "if" clause is technically called the *protasis.* After the protasis comes the consequence or penalty, called the *apodosis:* ". . . the accuser shall be put to death." Consider a few other examples from Hammurabi's code: "If a citizen breaks the bone of another citizen, they shall break his bone." "If a citizen hits the pregnant daughter of a citizen, and she has a miscarriage, the citizen shall pay ten shekels of silver for her miscarriage." The law codes of the Sumerians, the Assyrians, and the Hittites all follow this same basic structure.

These "if-then" laws are called *casuistic laws,* which simply means they're based on actual or hypothetical court cases. As new circumstances arise, the corpus of casuistic law expands to guide judges in making their decisions. In our own judicial system, we speak about "legal precedence." Decisions made in one court can become the standard by which other courts judge similar cases.

It's interesting to note that such laws don't explicitly state what one should or shouldn't do. Rather, they *assume* that certain things are wrong and outline how infractions should be handled. Consequently, case law can't operate in a moral vacuum. It needs a foundation of shared principles regarding what's right and what's wrong.

The books of Exodus, Leviticus, Numbers, and Deuteronomy (which, together with Genesis, comprise the section of the Bible known as the Pentateuch) contain many laws of this type. Right after the Ten

Commandments in Exodus 20, Exodus 21 begins, "These are the laws you are to set before them [i.e., the Israelites]: If you buy a Hebrew servant, he is to serve you for six years. . . ." And for the next chapter and a half, case laws are propounded. The word translated "laws" in this verse, *mishpatim*, actually means "judgments" or "legal rulings." So it might be more accurate to translate the verse, "These are the legal rulings you are to set before them." They're the judicial decisions that Israelite judges were to use in deciding the cases brought before them.

No doubt this part of the Law grew throughout the ages as circumstances changed and new judgments were made. Indeed, Moses himself established the pattern for adding to the case laws. Leviticus 24:10–23 records an incident in which a man, whose father was Egyptian, became angry and blasphemed the name of the Lord. An assembly was convened to decide what to do with him. Moses sought counsel from the Lord, and the Lord instructed Moses that the man should be stoned to death. A legal precedence was thereby established: Anyone who blasphemes the name of the Lord within the camp of Israel must be executed. In this manner, the casuistic laws could be a fluid body. As new situations arose, the judges would seek divine guidance in order to set legal precedents to which future generations could make reference.

THE FORM OF THE TEN COMMANDMENTS

The Ten Commandments, however, don't conform to the pattern of the case laws. Instead of the "if-then" formula, the Ten Commandments simply say, "do-don't." Such pronouncements don't occur in Hammurabi's Code, or any of the other ancient systems of law. It's unique to ancient Israel. Scholars call such law *apodictic*, meaning that it consists of authoritative pronouncements. The biblical designation for this style of law is "decree," a word that comes from the verb *hoq*, meaning to inscribe or engrave. Unlike judgments, which can change as new cases arise and new precedents are established, decrees are "engraved in stone." They arise not out of a courtroom, but out of God's direct commands to his people. Their main purpose isn't to guide judges in proper decisions, but to lay out before the people what God expects of them.

The difference between "judgments" and "decrees" becomes especially clear when we look at the last commandment—"You shall not covet" (Exod. 20:17). This matter of coveting—wanting something that isn't yours—is hardly the kind of thing that's dealt with in the courts. How would a police officer know whether or not someone was coveting something? What kind of evidence would a prosecutor present to argue a case against the accused? Obviously, this commandment couldn't be a "law" in the usual sense of the word. It's unenforceable. Furthermore, the Ten Commandments don't prescribe penalties for the offenses they prohibit. Without prescribed penalties, the Ten Commandments alone would be practically useless as a law code.

It seems likely, then, that the Commandments were never intended to serve as a law code *per se*. Rather, it's better to think of them as vows—vows defining the special relationship between God and his people. It was a relationship established back in the days of Abraham, when the Lord made a promise to the Patriarch that he would multiply his descendants, settle them in their own land, and make them a blessing to all peoples. The relationship was reaffirmed when the Lord sent Moses to Pharaoh in order to lead the Israelites out of slavery. The Israelites hadn't earned God's deliverance. It was only God's promises to the patriarchs that obligated him to deliver the people of Israel.

When Moses brought the people to Mount Sinai, the relationship entered into its second phase. God's promises to Abraham had been unconditional. The Lord swore to fulfill them, no matter what Abraham or his descendants might do. In the new phase of the relationship, some "give and take" was required. On Mount Sinai, God entered into a pact with the Israelites. "You yourselves have seen what I did to the Egyptians," he said, "and how I bore you on eagles' wings, and brought you to Myself" (Exod. 19:4 NASB). With these words, God reminded the Israelites of his matchless power—and that he exercised that power on Israel's behalf. Then he set before Israel the conditions of this new covenant: "If you will indeed obey My voice and keep My covenant, then you shall be My own possession among all the peoples" (19:5 NASB).

The Lord vowed that he would be Israel's God, that he would bring them into the Promised Land, and that he would always defend them against their enemies. Israel would be blessed with life, with health, and with prosperity—but there was a price. If the Lord was going to be for Israel, then Israel must be for the Lord. The people took a vow to follow God's requirements, and thereby to be set apart from the other nations of world (see also Deut. 6-7). The most basic vows—the summary that captured the essence of all that was required—were the Ten Commandments.

The Ten Commandments, then, rather than a collection of laws for ordering a just society, more closely resemble marital vows. Like marriage vows, they lay out the obligations of the parties involved in a committed relationship. Also like marriage vows, the sanctity of the relationship would be violated if the Israelites failed to honor their commitment. And like marriage vows, the Ten Commandments laid out only the essentials for a happy relationship with God. The details were filled in later, in the case laws and the other biblical decrees that followed in the rest of the Pentateuch.

In view of the changeable, evolving nature of "case law," the necessity of these concrete decrees is especially clear. The decrees—the vows—form the unchanging moral basis for the law code. New situations would require that new laws be composed. As Israel settled down into her land, as she became a nation and began to deal with foreigners, as new technologies were developed, there would be new laws written. But the firm foundation of those laws would be the unchanging decree of God, summarized in the Ten Commandments.

DIFFERENT VERSIONS OF THE COMMANDMENTS

Before looking at the laws themselves, we must consider the fact that the Ten Commandments are preserved in slightly different forms in several different places. The first location, the one we're most familiar with, is Exodus 20:1-17. In Deuteronomy 5:6-21, the Ten Commandments are stated again in very similar language. Here, Moses repeats the commandments in a speech wherein he emphasizes the importance of obedience to God. Exodus 34 relates that God gave

Moses a second set of tablets bearing the Ten Commandments to replace those that Moses had broken when he came down from Sinai the first time (Exod. 32:19). Exodus 34 contains slightly different versions of the first, second, and fourth commandments, but it doesn't list all ten of them as Exodus 20 and Deuteronomy 5 do. Finally, Leviticus 19 contains several of the commandments in different forms. The commandments regarding the Sabbath day and parents are briefly stated in 19:3; the prohibition of idols is found in 19:4; the prohibition of stealing is in 19:11. Verses 11 and 12 seem to expand on the commandment, "Do not bear false witness."

A lot of speculation has arisen on how these different versions of the commandments came into being. Some scholars believe that they represent different strains of tradition. One version might have circulated in the north while another circulated in the south. They were later brought together by the person who was responsible for the final form of the first five books of the Bible. Other scholars argue that the commandments were repeated in slightly different forms simply to more strongly drive home their message. For our purposes here, however, the issue of why the different versions exist is irrelevant. What's important is the ability to cross-reference them in order to comprehend how these commandments were understood by the ancient Israelites.

Understanding what these ancient commandments meant for the Israelites is the first step to understanding what they mean for Christians today. Unless we understand the historical significance of the commandments, we can't appreciate the principles behind them, and we can't fully experience the power they possess in helping us to grow into the image of Christ.

QUESTIONS FOR REFLECTION

1. Do the similarities between the ancient law codes and the Old Testament laws make you uncomfortable? Why or why not?
2. What is the basis for the authority of law in our society? How do you think society would be different if our laws derived their authority from the Bible or from some other "divine" authority (for instance, the Koran)?

3. Can you think of situations where apodictic (decree) law would be more useful than casuistic (case) law? Where casuistic law would be more useful than apodictic law?

4. Which do you believe are more powerful—laws or vows? People often violate their marriage vows, but most don't seriously break the law. Why is this so?

5. How would you explain the different forms of the Ten Commandments found in Exodus, Leviticus, and Deuteronomy?

three

God and the Gods

I am the LORD *your God, who brought you out of the land of Egypt, out of the house of slavery. You shall have no other gods before Me.*
—Exodus 20:2 NASB

IN THE FIRST CHAPTER, it was argued that we should seek to live not by the letter of the Ten Commandments, but according to the principles behind the commandments. Each commandment must be considered in its historical and biblical context in order to determine what principle the commandment embodies. When we think of the Ten Commandments as marriage vows, rather than a set of laws, the principle behind the first commandment, "You shall have no other gods before me," is immediately apparent. Just as a good marriage is founded on mutual commitment and trust, so must the relationship between Israel and her God be based on exclusive commitment. God is saying to Israel, "If this relationship is going to work, we have to establish some ground rules. The first ground rule is this: I am your God. Period. I brought you out of Egypt to make you my people. No other god has a claim on you as solid as my claim. So you aren't to have any other gods."

Some people have considered the phrase "before me" a bit vague. In English, it usually means that no one else can come first, but it doesn't mean that no others can come after. If that were case, the

Lord wouldn't be demanding the exclusive devotion of Israel, just their primary devotion: "Serve any gods you want, as long as you take care of your obligation to me first." Or, to use the marriage metaphor, "Go ahead, dear. Have all the husbands you want! Just as long as my dinner is on the table when I get home."

The permissive interpretation fails on two counts. First, it's not the most likely linguistic understanding of the original Hebrew text. The Hebrew preposition *liphne,* "before," can certainly mean "preceding," but it has a more basic and common meaning. Literally, it means "at my face," or "in my presence." So God isn't saying, "Have all the gods you want, as long as I come first"; rather, he's saying "I don't want any other gods in my presence." The second problem is that there's no evidence supporting the more permissive interpretation anywhere else in the Old Testament. No passage in the entire Bible implies that the worship of gods other than the Lord is acceptable. Polytheism (multiple god worship) was a reality in ancient Israel, but it's always regarded as sinful.

To us today, this commandment sounds simple to obey. In modern American society there's not much temptation to worship strange deities. But consider the ancient Israelites. The ancient Near East was a land of many gods—many, many gods. Gods were frequently regarded as the epitomes of some natural force or occurrence. Baal, the chief god of the Canaanites and the Syrians, was the personification of the earth's fertility. He brought the rains that fertilized the earth and made the crops grow. Marduk, the chief Babylonian god, was a storm god; and Shamash of the Babylonians and the Moabites was the god of the sun and the giver of justice. Molek, god of the Ammonites, was what we call a "chthonic" deity. He was the god of the underworld who reigned over the dead. Dagan, head of the Philistines' pantheon, was a grain god. Ashtoreth or Ishtar, worshiped throughout the Near East (and Greece and Rome, as well), was the goddess of love and war, responsible for the fertility of the soil, the giving of children, and success in battle. There were also minor deities who were invoked to aid in childbirth, to turn aside sickness, or to avert a locust plague. Gods were all very specialized in those ancient times, and different deities were shared by many different nations.

With such a variety of gods, how did people know which ones they were to worship? Most peoples worshiped a national god that was believed to be the patron of that nation. This national god received the most lavish temples and the biggest sacrifices on national holidays. National gods, however, didn't receive a guaranteed tenure. They had to prove themselves by bringing the nation victory in war and providing general security. Sometime shortly before biblical times, Syria had switched its main allegiance from the god El to the god Baal; during the reign of Nabonidus, Babylon briefly switched allegiance from Marduk to the moon goddess Sin. For the most part, however, the national god was well-established in its position and was adored by all the people of the nation.

Worshipers did not generally consult these national gods with the trivia of daily life. The gods were too busy running the country to be concerned about the average Joe or Jane. And so, the national gods had many helpers who saw to the mundane tasks like making the crops grow or helping someone win big at gambling. Even though persons might normally be devotees of Baal, they might pray to the god Bes when about to give birth, or to Shamash when going to court. Furthermore, many people had a personal or household god that they relied on as their "go between" to intercede between themselves and the big gods. (In Israel, such personal gods were represented by the *teraphim*, as mentioned in 1 Samuel 19:13.) So people had not one god but many. In addition, when traveling in a foreign land, it was customary to pay homage to the god of that land. The national gods were considered to be especially watchful over their territories, and one didn't want to offend the local deity by an act of thoughtlessness.

Given this kind of cultural setting, it's no wonder that the Israelites might have found the first commandment hard to swallow. How could the Lord ask the people to give up all their other deities and worship him alone? Were they supposed to pray to him for *everything*? Could the common person pray to the Lord, just as the priest and king would do? Could God possibly hear them all at the same time? Would he really *want* to be bothered with the minor details of daily life? What did the Lord know about childbirth? What would he know about farming, living as he did up there on barren Mount Sinai. Wasn't the Lord demanding too much—putting a burden on himself and his people?

So you can see why a commandment that sounds like a piece of cake to us might have been hard to swallow in ancient times. God demanded that the Israelites look to him for everything, to turn to him alone in every situation. But in return for the Israelites' exclusive worship, God promised to supply everything they needed. The Lord was asking for complete trust from Israel, but it wasn't blind trust. He had already demonstrated in the exodus from Egypt his ability to take care of his people. Through the plagues that Moses brought on Pharaoh, God demonstrated that he was superior to the whole legion of Egypt's gods. Furthermore, God had demonstrated his exclusive love for Israel. Though all the earth belongs to the Lord, Israel would be his special possession—as long as he was exclusively *theirs*. It was a radical departure from ancient tradition and truly made Israel unique among the nations.

PROVOKING GOD TO JEALOUSY

When we think of the Ten Commandments as similar to marriage vows, we get a better appreciation of another aspect of Israel's relationship with her God: God's "jealousy," his longing to possess Israel as his exclusive mate. The second commandment explicitly states that if the Israelites make idols or images of heavenly bodies or other created things, God will be provoked to jealousy (Exod. 20:5). These idols don't represent the Lord alone. They also represent rival deities, gods who would be consulted for help in various situations alongside or instead of the Lord. God's jealousy is explored more thoroughly in Exodus 34:10-16. Here, God states that those who worship other gods "prostitute themselves" with them—they're not keeping their marital covenant pure. Like any good husband who truly cares for his wife, God will become jealous; not because he's a mean-spirited, insecure tyrant who wants to keep his bride barefoot and pregnant. Rather, he's a devoted husband who gives himself exclusively to his wife and expects the same level of devotion from her.

Sad to say, Israel often failed to keep the relationship so pure. The

Old Testament tells many stories of how the nation strayed after other gods. When Israel settled in the Promised Land, they were attracted to Baal, the lascivious god of the Canaanites (Judg. 2:10-23). The sexual rites that were involved in Baal worship had a certain attraction to the Israelites' baser human instincts. Later, when Solomon was king, he married many foreign princesses in order to cement his political alliances. These women brought their alien gods and their priests with them. Many people of Israel were drawn into their snare, provoking the Lord to judge the nation (1 Kings 11:1-13). God set events in order so that civil war ensued, dividing the Israelites into two nations—Israel in the north and Judah in the south. Even after this judgment, the apostasy continued.

While the Israelites were pursuing their foreign gods, the prophets tried to remind them of the covenant they had made with God at Sinai—a covenant the seers characterized as a marriage. Jeremiah compared Israel and Judah to faithless wives who commit adultery with multiple lovers, symbolized by the many gods they worshiped (Jer. 3:1-20). In Isaiah 54, God speaks of Israel as his wife, a faithless wife whom he had abandoned because of her sins. But now, he says, in spite of Israel's many infidelities, he is willing to forgive her and take her back.

The book of the prophet Hosea, however, provides the most explicit and pathetic exploration of the marriage theme. In Hosea 1-3, God commanded the prophet to marry a prostitute, take her from the streets and care for her. Hosea's marriage was to be a symbol of God's relationship with Israel. So Hosea married a woman named Gomer, who bore him two sons. But Gomer never gave up her immoral sideline of adultery and prostitution, just as Israel continued in adulterous relations with foreign gods. The narrative isn't clear on what happens next, but it appears that Hosea divorced his wife for a time. Later, God commanded him to return to her and marry her once again. Hosea actually had to pay money to reclaim his wayward ex-spouse. The lesson is clear: just as Hosea continued to love Gomer in spite of herself, God had remained devoted to faithless Israel, and wanted to reclaim her as his bride.

In the Old Testament, God's love for Israel is different from his love for any other people of the earth. Even though all the world belongs to God, even though he hates nothing that he has made, he has a special love for those counted among his chosen ones (Exod. 19:4-6). From them, he expects a complete commitment. They are bound to him, and him only, by a sworn covenant. This is no "open marriage," no polygamous relationship. God's people are to worship no other gods, and he in return will care for them as he cares for no other people.

Remember that this marriage analogy is only that—it's an analogy designed to help us understand our relationship with God. On the one hand, analogies aren't perfect; if we try to push them too far, they can mislead us. But on the other hand, the principle expressed by the analogy isn't imperfect. God's people exist in an exclusive, committed relationship with the Lord. No other gods will be tolerated.

PLURALISM IN MODERN SOCIETY

The situation in modern Western society is rather different from the one in ancient Israel. Most people don't worship a bevy of gods or think of gods as specialists to be consulted only on matters related to their unique interests and abilities. We aren't faced with the temptation to give the Lord the second or third spot on our list of preferred deities.

Yet modern society presents a different set of dilemmas regarding the first commandment. We live in closer contact with people of different religions than ever before. Our neighbors may be Jewish, Hindu, Buddhist, or nothing at all. I once enjoyed a most unusual Thanksgiving dinner at my neighbor's home. He was Hindu, his wife was Christian, and some of the friends in attendance were Muslims. This scenario is not entirely unique. According to some polls, there are now more Muslims and Buddhists in the United States than there are Episcopalians.

In a society such as ours, we need to be understanding and respectful regarding other peoples' beliefs. Tolerance has become a cardinal virtue for us, as it has been for no other people in history. Christians who openly mock non-Christian religions are considered insensitive and bigoted. For many of us, then, the first commandment raises two troubling issues. First, given the existence of so many different religions, can we really believe that God has an exclusive relationship with just one chosen people? Isn't it possible that we all just worship the same God in different ways? And second, given the fact that we rub shoulders with people of different faiths almost every day, how can we build bridges of trust and understanding with them, and yet not violate the first commandment? Let's deal with these two questions in order.

AN EXCLUSIVE RELATIONSHIP WITH GOD?

Even though it may seem like society has changed greatly, the question of God's exclusive relationship with his chosen people is really no more of an issue for us today than it was in ancient times. There have always been people with different beliefs living in close company to each other. In the days of the Neo-Babylonian Empire (sixth century B.C.), when many religions were brought together under the same government and in the same land, some ancient (non-Jewish) religious texts express ideas that almost sound modern. They argue that all religions basically worship the same god, only under different names. In the Hellenistic era, when the Greeks had conquered the Near East (after 332 B.C.), the Jews were considered rather narrow-minded because they insisted that only their religion was true. The Jews wouldn't take part in "ecumenical" events where different gods were honored. So the problems of our new pluralistic society really *aren't* new. The first commandment wasn't given because God was ignorant or naive about the existence of other religions. Indeed, the opposite is true. It was because of the other religions that the first commandment was necessary.

The Israelites recognized the substantial differences between their God and the gods of other religions. The Lord is not a god of mythical tales, a capricious tyrant, or a lecherous old man. He's not bound to a specific geographic area, nor is he a specialist in a certain aspect of nature. He is God the Creator, maker of heaven and earth. Other gods were therefore lesser gods.

Today, substantial differences still exist between the gods of different world religions and the God of the Christian faith. We shouldn't take comfort in the modern myth that all religions are basically the same. They're basically different, because their concepts of God are different. In Buddhism, the concept of god is impersonal and ill-defined—one can be a good Buddhist and believe in no god at all. In Hinduism, god is conceived as a pantheon, a multifaceted being that encompasses every aspect of existence, both good and evil. In Islam, Allah is often viewed as the cause of all that happens. Though personal, Allah is almost equivalent to fate. A Muslim rarely thinks of God as "Father." Clearly, these concepts of deity are quite different from each other. We aren't all worshiping the same personal, loving Parent who became human in order to seek and save the lost world.

It is these differences that make the matter of pluralism so difficult. If we argue that our concept of God is correct, we also argue that other concepts are wrong. We say that God has revealed truth to some people, while leaving others in darkness. Could a good God act in such an "unfair" manner? It's a troubling, difficult question, and there may be no completely satisfying answer. But, the fact is, the Bible does give a little insight into this matter.

In the first chapters of his epistle to the Romans, Paul makes a few brief remarks about the Gentiles who haven't received the revelation of God through the Scriptures. Paul argues that much can be known about God through nature alone, and the Gentiles who act in accord with the law of God revealed in nature would be accepted by God (Rom. 1:18-20; 2:12-15). He also observes that the Gentiles usually turn away from the truth of God as revealed in nature, creating idols and engaging in abominable behavior (1:21-32). Because at least some truth can be known through "natural revelation," God is justified in condemning those who have not received the Scriptures and persist in sinfulness.

It would seem, then, that even those who don't have the Scriptures are not completely without the light of truth. God can have a unique relationship with one people without leaving the rest totally in the dark. The real issue is whether or not they embrace the light that has been revealed to them.

Another important consideration in the matter of pluralism is the mission of God's people. The Israelites were not instructed to keep the truth of God's word to themselves alone. Rather, they were called to be a "kingdom of priests" before the other nations. Since priests were intermediaries between God and humanity, no doubt this calling involved some missionary work on Israel's part. We find Israel functioning in this manner in the Old Testament more often than most people realize. Rahab, the harlot of Jericho (Josh. 2; 6:22-25), and Ruth, the grandmother of King David (Ruth 1:16; 2:12), were both proselytes to the Israelite religion. Naaman, who was healed of leprosy, was also a proselyte (2 Kings 5:17-18). The prophets looked forward to a day when Israel would be a light to the nations, spreading the Word of God throughout the earth (Isa. 60:1-3). In the New Testament, too, the church is charged to take the gospel to all the nations of the world (Matt. 28:19-20; Acts 1:8). God doesn't restrict truth to only a chosen few. If there are other religions, it's not because God wills it to be so. Rather, it's because we haven't fulfilled our mission to take the gospel to all people so they might hear and believe in Christ.

In the final analysis, the argument concerns the nature of truth. We want to believe that people with different viewpoints can all be right—and on some issues, they certainly can. I can say "toe-MAY-toe" and you might say "toe-MAH-toe," and we can simply agree to disagree. We may disagree on the significance of a historical event or the meaning of a work of art. Some matters don't have a definite right and wrong answer. But if we're driving down the road and I say the traffic light is red and you say it's green, we could be heading for an accident.

If the truth about God falls in the category of debatable issues, we'd all be better off just leaving each other alone. The Bible's point of view would be no better than any other. But the Bible doesn't present its revelation as if it were one possibility of many. Jesus said, "I am the way and the truth and the life. No one comes to the Father except through me" (John 14:6). John writes, "He who has the Son has life; he who does not have the Son of God does not have life" (1 John 5:12). Indeed, the fact that the Bible commands us to teach our faith to others shows that our biblical faith can't be regarded as one option out of many. If we choose to believe that our religion is just one way of looking at God, no better or worse than any other, we aren't holding to the faith of the Bible. We're creating a religion of our own, separate from the biblical revelation.

So unless we're inclined to disregard both the Old and New Testaments, and to overlook the observable differences between the major religions, we must deal with the fact that God has a unique relationship with his chosen people. Those chosen ones are none other than those who respond in faith to the revelation given in the Scriptures—the revelation that points us ultimately to Jesus Christ.

THE FIRST COMMANDMENT AND THE ECUMENICAL SPIRIT

If all the world's religions aren't just worshiping the same God under different names and guises—if there really are different "gods" out there, either literally or only in people's beliefs—then the first commandment has lost none of its validity for us today. In theory, at least, we could be drawn into the worship of other gods. In this day of ecumenical fervor, it's common for Christians to take part in religious services where people of many different faiths are present. I have Christian friends and relatives who've taken part in Buddhist meditation groups, in Shinto tea ceremonies, and in Native American religious rituals. We might well wonder, have they broken the first commandment?

In a literal sense, it seems they have. But it has been argued in an earlier chapter that we must look beyond the facile, literal interpretation of the Old Testament laws to the principle that lies beneath. As we've already seen, the principle at work in this first commandment is one of maintaining an exclusive, committed relationship between God and God's people. Some might say that God is only concerned about our devotion, not our motions. One can certainly go through the motions of a religious ritual—whether those rituals be Christian or pagan—without having one's heart in the least engaged.

In 2 Kings 5, for example, a man named Naaman, commander in the army of the pagan Arameans, came to the prophet Elisha seeking a cure for his leprosy. When he was cured, he pledged to worship the

God of Israel and not the gods of the Arameans. But Naaman had a problem. His position required him to go with the king to the temple of the pagan god Rimmon and bow down there before the idol. Naaman asked that he would be forgiven this "transgression." Elisha was quite willing to forgive him since the action was empty. It meant nothing because Naaman's heart wasn't in it.

In the days of the Roman Empire, the church had a similar problem. How was it to deal with Christians who, under the threat of death, had burned incense to the image of the Emperor, but now wanted to be restored to the fellowship of the church? Most church leaders were willing to receive them back into full fellowship. It was decided that merely participating in the actions of a non-Christian worship ceremony doesn't necessarily constitute a violation of the first commandment.

Another analogy might be helpful. I often treat myself to wholesome old movies, full of drama and romance. Is it possible that the two actors on screen could pledge their love to each other, hold one another, even kiss, and yet not feel the slightest romantic attraction to each other? Under such circumstances, only a complete prude would think of accusing the actors of committing adultery with each other through their on-stage actions. (The torrid, no-holds-barred scenes in some modern films constitute a different matter entirely.) In such cases, the actors' bodies may go through the motions of romance, but the heart is not involved. In the same fashion, someone could go through the rituals of pagan worship without ever compromising his or her relationship with the living God.

We might question the wisdom of such actions, however, on the same basis that Paul cautions those who eat meat in pagan temples (1 Cor. 10:23–33). We should avoid anything that might cause another to stumble in his or her faith. If a non-Christian were to see a Christian taking part in a pagan ritual, he or she might well conclude that Christians find non-Christian religions acceptable. Our position as ambassadors of a better faith, a truer hope, would be dangerously compromised. Heaven help us if our glib participation in a non-Christian ritual, however innocent in our eyes, caused a Christian brother or sister to abandon the gospel to follow an Eastern guru.

Many eyes are watching us, and watching especially those who are considered more mature or strong in their Christian faith. So while my Christian friends may not have violated the first commandment by participating in non-Christian rituals, it might have been better had they abstained.

SAINTS AS SUBSTITUTES FOR GOD

Another practice—actually a quite ancient one—that also should be considered in light of the first commandment is the adoration of saints and angels. The practice of praying to saints and angels goes back to the Middle Ages. It was strongly condemned by the Protestant Reformers and seemed for many centuries to be confined to Catholic and Orthodox circles. But with the growing hunger for spirituality and tradition that marked the end of the twentieth century, saints and angels have enjoyed widespread attention.

I have no intention of debating here the merits of venerating saints and angels. The Bible nowhere condemns such a practice, but neither does it condone it. It would be necessary to look beyond specific Bible texts and consider our understanding of the nature of prayer, the role of angels, and our conceptions of the afterlife in order to explore properly whether saints and angels can hear prayers. Such an exercise is far afield of the present task. It is worthy, however, to question whether such a practice can lead us to violate the first commandment.

As already seen, the principle behind the first commandment is one of devotion to a relationship. The loyalty that is due to God must not be divided with any other deity. Obviously, saints and angels aren't gods, in the strict sense of the word. Even the people who hold them in the highest regard generally keep that distinction clear in their minds. But is it possible that saints and angels might nonetheless supplant God—at least partially? And by supplanting God, do they, themselves, become for us "gods"? The ancient Hebrew word for both "God" and "gods," *elohim,* doesn't designate a supernatural being only. Its basic meaning is "mighty one." In the Bible, it's used not only for the Lord and pagan deities, but also at times to designate angels or even human magistrates (Pss. 82:1, 6; 138:1). So then, the wording of the first commandment needn't be restricted to prohibiting foreign deities alone. "No other gods" may well have a wider application to anything that exercises godlike influence.

Indeed, some Christians seem to attribute such influence to saints and angels. In biblical times, you'll remember, there were different gods responsible for various earthly realms. People would consult certain gods for success in war, others for help in childbirth, and others for the growth of their crops. The main god or national deity was usually consulted only by priests or only for major concerns. Angels and saints are sometimes given similar treatment today. Saints are often considered to have specialized areas of responsibility or particular talents, just like the gods in the ancient pantheons. Some people will pray to St. Anthony to help them find a lost object, to St. Jude for a child's healing, and to St. Christopher to protect them while traveling.

Two ideas contribute to this behavior. One is that specialists are more suited to handle problems than generalists. A podiatrist is more suited to handle our ingrown toenails than our family doctor would be. Appealing to a spiritual specialist, however, demonstrates a subtle lack of faith in God's omnipotence. Our all-knowing, all-loving heavenly Father is surely more qualified to deal with whatever affliction I might have than any saint or angel, no matter how lofty their expertise. God is not only the Jack-of-All-Trades; he's also the Master of All.

The other contributing idea is that our earthly hierarchical systems also operate in heaven. God has so much to worry about, some think, that he delegates the smaller matters to saints and angels. Thus, one might say, "I don't want to bother God when I've lost my car keys, but bothering a saint is a different matter—it's his *job* to help me find them." Again, this attitude shows the same lack of trust in God's power, but it also may arise from not considering God's great love. Jesus said that our Father in heaven marks the fall of every sparrow (Matt. 10:29–31). He doesn't entrust the task to the Bureau of Sparrow Population Statistics. How much more valuable are we to him than sparrows?

The truth is, God wants us to bother him with the little things as well as with the big things. He longs for us to bring all our problems to him: "Cast all your anxiety on him because he cares for you" (1 Peter 5:7).

Some Christians find the thought of coming directly to God intimidating. But Jesus died to give us that right of direct access. His death on the cross provides us free entry into the very presence of God, making all believers priests before God and children of God. When Jesus died, the veil in the temple that separated the worshipers from their God, that hid God's presence from their view, was miraculously torn in half (Matt. 27:51). Clearly, this act was a sign that we now have direct access into the presence of the Lord. Christ himself became the veil, the only intermediary between us and the Father (Heb. 10:19–22). It was this principle of direct access that drove the Protestant Reformation, which stands as the very foundation for our modern Christian faith.

It's possible, then, that when some Christians pray to a saint instead of praying to God, they miss out on the intimacy with God the Creator that is supposed to be theirs through Jesus Christ. In such a case, they surely compromise their relationships with God. They're giving someone else the devotion and responsibility that's due to God. By so doing, they set, to a greater or lesser degree, a God-substitute in God's place. They stand in violation of the first commandment.

OTHER SUBSTITUTES FOR GOD

Saints and angels are beings whom we may allow to come between us and God. But God-substitutes might also be *things* that keep us from giving God the love and respect that is his due. Martin Luther once said, "Whatever your soul clings to and relies upon, that is your god." With this statement, Luther gives the concept of God a subjective definition rather than merely an objective one—a basis in us, rather than the object of consideration. Luther's statement also reminds me of something I was told many years ago by Sunday school teachers who had never even heard of Martin Luther: "Anything in your life that you value more than God is really your god." I was warned that if I gave more attention to my bicycle than I did to my Bible, I was guilty of breaking the first commandment.

These statements have the ring of truth, but they need additional scrutiny. Is the love for or value that we place on something criterion enough to make it our "god"? If Abraham, for example, had decided that he wasn't able to sacrifice his son Isaac, that he loved Isaac more than he loved the Lord, would Isaac have become Abraham's god? I don't think so. In itself, our love for something doesn't make it our god. Power—the ability to influence—is the main criterion for divinity. So a thing's "god status" would be determined by its subjective influence over us. While there's no doubt that the people and things I love can deeply influence me, they don't necessarily control me.

No, the principle qualification for a god is not that it be loved, but that it is powerful. Remember, the Hebrew word for "gods" comes from a root meaning "mighty." It isn't the thing to which we give love that necessarily becomes our object of worship, but that to which we give authority. There's nothing inherently divine about an image made out of wood (even if we believe that it represents a spirit). It's just a piece of wood carved into some unusual shape. As the book of Isaiah observes, the carver may well have used some of the same log for his fireplace and some of it to bake his bread (Isa. 44:12-20). Only the idolaters' attitude toward the image—their devotion to and dependence upon it—makes the object their god. They themselves grant it the authority to be their deity. So it would seem that Martin Luther is right when he defines a god as that to which we cling and on which we rely. There's nothing necessarily godlike in our God-substitutes, except our reliance on them.

People can cling to and rely on many things. Money, of course, is the most obvious example. Once, in high school, I pulled a dollar bill out of my wallet and cleaned my glasses with the beautiful, lint-free paper. The teacher saw me wiping my lenses and reacted with indignation. "If you haven't got any more respect for money than that," he fumed, "why don't you just give it to me?" You'd have thought I'd desecrated a temple. Indeed, some people regard money with an almost superstitious awe. They're sure there's no problem in their lives or in society that money can't solve. They look not to the Lord as their protector but to their bank account balances, their stock portfolios, or their insurance policies. Their energy is devoted to the pursuit of money, their time to its accumulation. It's another god, the god "Mammon," set up beside the Lord. Surely, this lofty regard is a violation of the first commandment.

Others give their devotion and reliance to other people. "Co-dependents," for example, rely so completely on other individuals that they will often remain in unhealthy or abusive relationships rather than face the prospect of being alone. While all of us at times cling to others for emotional support, codependents do so to a much greater degree. They are emotionally crippled, often requiring extensive counseling in order to overcome their disabling reliance. They're making another person into a God-substitute and living in violation of the first commandment. God can provide them with strength to escape from their addictive lifestyles. They must recognize that their dependence isn't just unhealthy, it's sinful as well.

Many more God-substitutes could be identified. Some people have trusted in military might as a god, relying on force to provide them safety and security. Others use sex to fill the emptiness in their lives. Some have even treated the church as if it were a god, giving it their allegiance, trusting in its power, loving its organization and causes, while neglecting its Lord. Anything that we elevate in our minds to a place of Godlike authority will separate us from the Lord, adulterate our relationship with the true God, and cut us off from the blessings that he wants us to enjoy in our relationship with him.

THE FIRST COMMANDMENT AND THE GREAT COMMANDMENT

When Jesus was asked what was the greatest commandment of all, he replied, "Love the Lord your God with all your heart and with all your soul and with all your mind" (Matt. 22:37). Jesus was quoting Deuteronomy 6:5, part of a Scripture passage known to the Jewish people as the *Shema'*, or "Hear!" The *Shema'* begins "Hear, O Israel: The LORD [Yahweh] is our God, the Lord alone!" (Deut. 6:4, author's translation). These verses have come to be regarded as the basic creed of Judaism, the epitome of what it means to believe the Jewish faith.

From what we've discussed above, it's clear that these words also capture the principle behind the first commandment. We should have no God but the Lord. We are bound to him by a love that will admit no rivals, divine or otherwise. So the first commandment is essentially the Great Commandment as well. An unalloyed, unrestricted love, freely flowing between us and our heavenly Father, fulfills the requirement of the Law.

QUESTIONS FOR REFLECTION

1. How might the marriage analogy help us understand our relationship with God? How might the analogy not be helpful?
2. Do you see any advantages in worshiping many gods as opposed to one God? One God, as opposed to many?
3. Do you think there can be opposing truths on the same issue? How might our knowledge of God be open to different interpretations and still reflect a single truth?
4. Do you ever feel reluctant to bring your "little" needs before God? Why or why not? Do you think saints can hear our prayers?
5. Are there any things in your own life that could become "God-substitutes"? How can you deal with the temptation of putting other people or things before the Lord?

f o u r

Serving Gods We Can See

You shall not make for yourself an idol in the form of anything
in heaven above or on the earth beneath or in the waters below.
You shall not bow down to them or worship them; for I, the LORD
your God, am a jealous God, punishing the children for the sin
of the fathers to the third and fourth generation of those who
hate me, but showing love to a thousand generations of those
who love me and keep my commandments.
—Exodus 20:4-6

BACK IN THE LATE 1970s, archaeologists made a remarkable discovery at a site known as Quntillet Ajrud, in the Sinai Peninsula. Three thousand years ago Quntillet Ajrud was the location of an Israelite copper mining town. Copper mining was a laborious and tedious occupation, engaged in by people who could not make a living in other ways. Thus, the inhabitants of Quntillet Ajrud were generally unsophisticated folks—slaves and hired hands from many backgrounds and nationalities. When the site was abandoned in the eighth century B.C., its inhabitants left behind their tools, their buildings, and some letters written on pieces of broken pottery.

The most interesting artifact was a potsherd bearing the inscription, "I bless you by Yahweh, God of Samaria, and his Asherah." (After Israel divided into two kingdoms, Samaria became the capital of the northern kingdom. Judah, the southern kingdom, had its capital at Jerusalem.) These words were scrawled above a crude picture depicting two obviously male deities standing before a seated goddess, who strummed a harp. Some scholars suggested two of the figures were meant to represent the Lord (Yahweh) and Asherah, the pagan fertility goddess.

The publication of this artifact set off an academic firestorm. Some scholars leapt to remarkable conclusions. This potsherd was proof, they said, that the ancient Israelites had worshiped a goddess alongside the Lord, and hadn't been the "exclusive monotheists" (worshipers of one God) that the Bible commands them to be. That revelation shouldn't, of course, have come as a great surprise. The Bible freely admits that the Israelites worshiped the goddess Asherah. Where the Bible would disagree with some of these modern scholars is on the matter of timing. The scholars argue that Israel was originally polytheistic, worshiping many gods, and later adopted monotheism. The Bible claims that Israel was originally monotheistic, worshiping the Lord alone, and later adopted the gods of the nations. The Quntillet Ajrud potsherd only demonstrates that foreign deities were worshiped in Israel. It has no implications at all about *when* they were first worshiped there.

So, it isn't the evidence of goddess worship in Israel that makes the Quntillet Ajrud inscription so interesting. Rather, the interesting thing is that in all the archaeological digs conducted in Israel, this one was the first to turn up anything that scholars suggest might be a picture of the Lord—and even here the the identification is dubious. On all the buildings, in all the homes, in the inscriptions on the walls and in digs at the temple mount, no other picture or statue has been found that can be identified as a depiction of Yahweh, God of Israel. It seems, then, that the majority of Israelites were very careful to observe the second commandment and make no images of the Lord. So conscientious were they about this commandment that in Jesus' time, the Jews wouldn't allow *any* images of people or animals to adorn their temple. Shortly after the death of Herod the Great, a riot broke out in Judea over the presence of a Roman imperial eagle in front of the temple. The Jews argued that it violated their second commandment.

IMAGES IN ANTIQUITY

This avoidance of images made the Jews truly unique in the ancient world. All nations had idols or images of some sort. Among the Egyptians and the people of India, gods were usually represented in the form of animals. These animals represented various aspects of nature or the created world that were epitomized by the animal image. The ancient Egyptians revered Horus, god of the sky, in the form of a falcon that flies high in the heavens. Khephri, god of the morning sun, was pictured as the scarab beetle, which the Egyptians believed came to life again like the rising sun.

In Greece, Rome, and the Near East, however, gods were never depicted as animals (even though they might at times be associated with various animals). Rather, the gods of these countries were depicted in human form. They were larger than life, to be sure, but human nonetheless. In the Near East, the gods were often pictured riding on the backs of their animal counterparts. El, chief god of Syria, was often called the Bull and was pictured riding on a bull or accompanied by a bull. The Bible tells us that the Israelites set up cow images in their shrines at Bethel and other places. Most likely, they didn't actually worship these cows. Rather, they regarded them as the mount on which God would sit when he came to visit the shrines. The cherubim—winged, human-headed lions—in the Jerusalem temple served much the same purpose. The presence of the Lord would descend upon these images and dwell there when God's presence met with his people.

The use of images to represent gods is understandable. People like having gods that they can relate to and that they feel can relate to them. We want to believe that our gods can understand us and sympathize with our situations. Our human tendency is to bring them down to our own level. The gods of Near Eastern and Greek mythology were just as petty, cruel, and lustful as the people over whom they supposedly ruled. They fought with each other, stole one another's wives and lovers, became drunk, sick, old, even impotent. The myths make interesting reading not because of their lofty theological ideas, but because of their very human pathos. One Greek philosopher observed that "The gods are immortal men." The main difference between us and them, it seemed, was that they lived forever. Even the supernatural powers they possessed were often ineffective when they had to deal with other gods or with the power of Fate.

Idols, in a sense, crystallize this tendency to humanize the divine. They make gods immanent, part of this world. We don't have to imagine the gods "out there" somewhere; the gods are here, with us, represented in the idol. The idolater usually realizes that an idol isn't his or her actual god. The idol represents the god, brings it close, into the temple or home. The idolater knows that the real god is in heaven somewhere. The idol merely makes that god more accessible to its worshiper. One can almost see a noble aspiration in idolatry—its purpose is to bring a worshiper closer to god.

The Israelites strongly avoided such images. As they understood it, the second commandment prohibited any kind of physical, man-made image of God. God could not be depicted as a man, a beast, or even (as was often the case in Persian art) a heavenly body, such as the sun, moon, or stars. No, the God of Israel was generally worshiped without images, the Quntillet Ajrud drawing being the possible exception to the rule. This absence of images so struck other nations in the ancient world that when the Greeks came into contact with the Jews in the fourth century B.C., rumors spread that the Jews were a nation of atheists. Since the Greeks saw no images, they inferred that the Jews had no gods.

Is God Invisible?

Our sophisticated modern minds might find the desire for a visible image of God a bit hard to grasp. After all, we think of God as an invisible Spirit. God doesn't have a body like you or I, so of course we couldn't draw a picture or make a sculpture of God. But that's a modern viewpoint. To the ancient mind, the ideas that God is Spirit and that God has physical form were not mutually exclusive. In fact, several Old Testament passages imply that God has a human form. When Moses asked to see the Lord, he was told that he couldn't see God's face—implying, of course, that God has a face. Moses was, however, allowed to see God's feet, legs, and back (Exod. 33:18-23; see also 24:10). In a vision, Isaiah saw the Lord as a king who was sitting on a throne and was dressed in royal robes (Isa. 6:1). When the Bible speaks of God's face, his hands, his arms, and his feet, we can't always dismiss the references as symbolic language. People in Old Testament times probably rarely questioned the assumption that God had a body and features much like their own. They might have taken the statement that human beings are made in God's image quite literally (Gen. 1:26-27). It was only much later that Jesus taught, "God is spirit, and his worshipers must worship in spirit and in truth" (John 4:24).

As theologians and philosophers have come to appreciate thinking of God as Spirit, we're led to believe that the Old Testament passages that speak about God's physical form are merely a concession to our limited human understanding. God manifested himself in ancient times in a form that the prophets and seers would have understood—usually, the form of a king, resplendent in his royal majesty. In the light of our deeper understanding of God through centuries of biblical revelation and reflection, we can recognize such images as metaphors—pictures that help us understand God's true nature. God rules the universe in the fashion of a king, but he mustn't be thought of as a literal king. God sits over creation like a king sitting in court, but the omnipotent Creator hardly needs a throne where he can rest his weary bones. Indeed, any bodily form is limiting. If God sees with eyes, then he can only see what's in front of his face and can't be all-knowing. If he needs legs with which to move from one place to another, then he isn't all-present. If he needs to hold things in his hands to manipulate them, he isn't all-powerful. If God has a physical form, then he isn't God in the sense we understand him to be.

Perhaps the second commandment anticipates this deeper understanding of God. Noting that the ancient Israelites accepted the idea that God would appear in human form, it's difficult to understand why God would forbid the Israelites from depicting him in that way. The Bible doesn't tell us why idols are wrong. It simply says, "Don't make an idol. Any idol."

Some scholars argue—contrary to the Jewish understanding of the verse—that this commandment prohibited only images of foreign deities rather than images of the Lord. The verse talks about heavenly bodies and other creatures that were commonly used by Israel's neighbors to represent gods. If the Israelites constructed images of such things to represent the foreign gods, they'd certainly be violating the first commandment and provoking God's jealousy (Exod. 20:5). Imagine how a man's wife would feel if her husband kept a photograph of a previous girlfriend on his office desk. So a prohibition of *pagan* idols is perfectly understandable under the principle of the first commandment. (Indeed, in the Roman Catholic Church, this second commandment is considered to be simply an extension of the first, and not a ban on images of the Lord at all. So they would have no objection to a painting of God in the Sistine Chapel.) But what harm could there be in a graven image of the Lord—especially when the Israelites seemed to conceive of God as having a physical form?

Perhaps the Israelites didn't know it at the time this commandment was given, but there are good reasons behind the biblical prohibition of idols. Some of the problems with idols are explicitly stated later in the Bible, and some we have to infer for ourselves. Let's consider a few of these issues.

IMAGES REFLECT HUMAN BIASES

What color is God? How tall is he? Is he male or female? What color are God's eyes and hair? If you're African, God's skin is probably dark brown. For the people of China, he has a definite Asian quality about him. In Michelangelo's famous Sistine Chapel painting, the arm that reaches down from heaven is as white as the European-looking Adam that God is creating. We definitely tend to project onto God the very features that we prize most in ourselves.

In the ancient Near East, the male deities were generally pictured as virile figures, well-muscled and full-bearded. Their great strength, skill in battle, and virility were celebrated in mythological stories. The goddesses were well-endowed women, large-breasted and full-hipped for the bearing of children. In ancient Greece, the finely chiseled features of Hermes, Apollo, and Aphrodite epitomize the Greek ideal of fit body and fit mind. Homer describes Hera, queen of the gods, with the epithet "cow-eyed"—considered a very attractive feature in ancient Greece. Zeus, king of the gods, is characterized by his massive size, overwhelming strength, and his curly black hair (of course, the king of the gods couldn't be balding). His extramarital sexual exploits are the theme of many a myth. A few of the gods were dwarves or misshapen, but these deities, rather than objects of adoration, were subjects of mocking stories. The important gods were good-looking, based on the standards of attractiveness in contemporary society.

Thus our images tend to embody the qualities that our society holds dear. In modern times, the venerable qualities of God as a great warrior (Exod. 15:3) and angry judge (Ps. 7:11; Ezek. 7:8) have been largely replaced by those traits that our own society values: a loving parent; a tolerant, forgiving friend; a cosmic administrator. Such qualities might well embody some aspects of God, but in reality they say more about our own natures than they do about the nature of God. The human tendency to perceive God as possessing human qualities prompted Karl Marx to view religion as friend of the status quo and opiate of the masses. A god who embodies the current values of society, he reasoned, must be overthrown if society is to embrace a new set of values.

But God is far more than the sum of our ideals and values. Indeed, God wants to transform our values, not embody them. Our society may value self-reliance and strength, but God wants us to learn humility and dependence. Society would make God a virile he-man, the very epitome of what many men would wish for themselves. But the Lord isn't interested in sexual conquest or in modeling predatory behavior. God's love is pure, unselfish, and untainted by a need for sexual gratification. If the God of the Bible were to be represented as having a wife or consort, we would without doubt project our fallen human sexuality on to the Lord.

Human beings tend to make God in their own image, but God wants to remake us into *his* image. He would challenge our personal and societal ideas of what is worthy and valuable, and destroy our false images of what is divine.

IDOLS CAN BE MANIPULATED

In ancient Babylon, the most significant religious event of the year was the *akitu,* or New Year's Festival. The long, elaborate ritual involved a reenactment of how Marduk, chief god of Babylon, triumphed over Tiamat, the ancient chaos monster. Marduk's image would be decorated with special ornaments for the festival. As the story of Marduk's battle was read before his idol, the faces of the idols Anu and Enlil, other Babylonian gods, were covered, symbolizing their subservience to Marduk. At one point in the ceremony, celebrants moved Marduk's statue to the Chamber of Destinies, thus signifying his right to renew the fruitfulness of the world for the coming year. The image was then carried in procession to the Festival House, where the primeval battle was reenacted. Eventually, the celebrants returned the idol to its temple, thereby indicating that Marduk was once again victorious over the forces of evil. And at no point in the ceremony did anyone ask, "Marduk, do you mind if I move your statue?"

An idol, then, is essentially at the mercy of its owners and worshipers. In the Old Testament, many stories record the less than respectful handling of idols by their worshipers. In one incident, Rachel steals the idols belonging to her father, Laban. When he comes to retrieve them, she hides them under her skirt and sits on them. (Gen. 31:19–35). Judges 17–18 relates the satirical story of a man named Micah, whose ironic name means, "Who is like the Lord?" Micah made images of the Lord with money he had stolen from his mother. He hired a wandering Levite to serve as priest in his makeshift shrine. A group of migrating Danites came upon Micah's shrine and were quite impressed by the idols and the priest. So they stole the idols, carried them off to Dan, their new homeland, and established the Levite and his descendants as their priests. In yet another case, King Saul sent soldiers to capture David, so Saul could kill him. David's wife, Michal, took the household idol and placed it in the bed and pulled the covers over its head, so that the soldiers would think David was ill in bed. When the soldiers returned without David, Saul sent them back to bring him, bed and all. Of course, they found only the idol (1 Sam. 19:11–17). The idol had been made party to a deception and was probably never consulted on the matter.

The Old Testament includes these stories without comment, but their message is clear. In a subtle lampoon, the stories reveal that idols are little more than props. They can be roughly handled by people who have no integrity or piety, and there's nothing the idols can do about it. Indeed, in ancient times when one nation conquered another, it was common practice for the idols of the conquered nation to be led out in chains as if they were prisoners of war. The chains were a sign that the gods of the vanquished nation had themselves been vanquished.

Even when idols are being treated with the utmost respect, as in the Babylonian *akitu* festival, they're still subject to human manipulation. We can paint a permanent smile on the face of our god and convince ourselves of its constant good will. We can pour juice or blood down their lifeless throats and be assured that our gifts have been accepted, because the idol doesn't spit it out. We can decorate them with fancy clothes and jewels, cover them with kisses, or hide them in the closet if we're doing something we don't want them to see. They can be taken from our shelves and paraded around in procession, made to fight imaginary battles, carried to thrones where they take their place in triumph. (Don't confuse processions of the Ark of the Covenant with these idol processions. The Ark was not an idol; it represented God's throne where God might—or might not—choose to make his presence manifest.) Idols can be manipulated, and people are quite good at convincing themselves that by doing so, they manipulate the deity as well. The fact that images are subject to human manipulation can have some disturbing results.

I recently read about one of the greatest flops in the history of the toy industry—the Jesus doll. The doll was about the size of a GI Joe, but it had ancient-looking garb and the long hair and features we've come to associate with the Lord Jesus. The manufacturer was sure the doll would go over well with millions of religious parents. But the few parents who bought the dolls ended up returning them to the store. The reasons? They didn't like their children taking Jesus' clothes off and leaving him lying around naked. Nor did they care for Jesus dating Barbie, riding in a dump truck, or dropping toy bombs on toy soldiers. The problems with images is that they tend to do whatever we *want* them to, whether they should be doing it or not.

And so, images are very different from the God we worship. God can't be manipulated by human beings as if he were a puppet on a string. We can ask God to bless us, or to heal our diseases, or to forgive our sins, but the initiative to do so always rests with God. Indeed, God's very unpredictability can try even the greatest of saints. St. Theresa once remarked to God that it was no wonder he had so few friends, considering how badly he treated them. In his *Chronicles of Narnia,* C. S. Lewis wrote of meeting the lion Aslan (who represents Christ in these stories), "Afraid? I should say you would be afraid. . . . After all, he's not a tame lion."

The idolater would bend the god to individual will, as if each individual knows what's best for him- or herself and for the world. But our God would have us learn to submit to his will, to trust him with our lives and destinies.

IDOLS ARE LIMITING

An apocryphal story has been circulating about a little child who was hard at work with her crayons. The mother observed her daughter's intense concentration and asked, "What are you drawing, honey?"

"I'm drawing God," the child replied.

"But dear," said the mother, "nobody knows what God looks like."

The child answered, "They will when I'm done!"

And so it is with many of us. We take our images of God so seriously that we run the risk of mistaking the images for the real thing. We can allow them to limit our concepts of God to the characteristics of our image. If our image is small, it's hard to conceive of a God who fills all earth and heaven. If the image is masculine, it's easy to forget that God is neither male nor female, but Spirit. If the image is white, we may find it difficult to believe that God is just as much the God of black, red, yellow, and brown peoples.

In Romans 1:22–25, Saint Paul alludes to the limitations of idols: "Although they claimed to be wise, they became fools and exchanged the glory of the immortal God for images made to look like mortal man and birds and animals and reptiles. . . . They exchanged the truth of God for a lie, and worshiped and served created things rather than the Creator—who is forever praised. Amen." God is immortal, but our images are all perishable. God is the Creator, but our images are all creations. Perhaps the philosophical idolater can look beyond the constraining image and capture some aspect of the limitless God, and perhaps not. In any case, he or she will only capture the aspects of God that the image can communicate—aspects that were selected by the crafter when the image was formed. How many images will it take to capture all of God?

Someone might well remark that none of us knows all of God all the time, or even part of the time. It might be well if some image could direct us to a deeper appreciation of just *one* aspect of God's nature. An Orthodox friend of mine tells me that using icons—pictures of Christ—has enriched her prayer life. They direct her to contemplate certain aspects of Christ's nature when she goes to prayer. For her, I'm sure that's good. But what if God wants to direct someone's attention to an aspect of his character that's not represented in the icon at hand? I can't speak to the Orthodox or Catholic experience, and I praise God if the use of icons has truly enriched the spiritual journey of many believers. But I question if icons would have the same enriching effect for every Christian. It seems likely that the use of images could limit one's prayer life, rather than enrich it.

No image we make with our hands, no picture we paint, no statue we cast could ever capture all of God's nature, or even a small part of God's nature. If images hinder us from seeing the unimaginable, less obvious, or even fearsome aspects of God's nature, they must be abandoned.

INTERNAL IMAGES

Undoubtedly, other objections could be raised against the use of idols. But the whole argument might seem academic. After all, no Christian would ever think of worshiping a statue, would they?

Yet the same objections to idols can be brought to bear against those images of God that are invisible—the images we carry around in our minds. Most of us have some impression about God that we keep in our minds when we pray, read the Bible, or worship. For many of us, that God-picture is a well-defined mental image. God may be a kindly old man, or the long-haired Jesus of our paintings, or a daunting king sitting on a throne. These images can play an important role in our Christian experience. They can help us to relate to God as a being—which, of course, he is—rather than an impersonal force. We'd have a much harder time relating to God if we pictured him as a mountain, or a bird, or the wind. These are all fine biblical images, but not ones that we can "cozy up" to very easily.

Our personal images of God, however, have the danger of becoming idols for us—self-constructed images that we can manipulate and that can limit the ways we view God. If our images become "set in stone," fixed and inflexible, they may even drive us away from the true God.

When I was in seminary, one of my professors, a pastor himself, told about a young woman he had counseled. Her problem was that she couldn't feel close to God. At times, she felt as if she hated him. The pastor asked her questions about her image of God, and discovered that her impression was primarily that of God as her father. When she prayed, it was her father's face she saw. When she read stories about God in the Bible, she projected her father into the role of God. The pastor then explored the young woman's relationship with her father, and learned about a history of physical and sexual abuse. No wonder the woman couldn't love God. She had been taught to think of God as her father, but to her, the father image implied all the things that God isn't—abusive, predatory, untrustworthy. How could she enjoy intimacy with her Creator when her image of God was so warped?

This young woman's experience dramatically illustrates the problem with mental images. Images of God can be comforting, helpful, and instructive, but they can also be destructive. An image that's cast in metal, set in stone, or set in our own minds is too constraining for our dynamic God. As a normal part of our Christian growth process, we must allow God to challenge our images—to shatter them, if necessary. As we encounter God in new ways, as we experience a fresh intimacy with the Creator, new aspects of God become real to us. If we insist on clinging to the old images, we may find that we don't have God at all—we have nothing but a cold, hard idol.

In His Image

Finally, let's consider an image of God that isn't obvious to most of us. It's interesting that the Old Testament tolerates only one *material* image of God. That image is the human being. God made humanity in his own image, giving us dominion over the earth (Gen. 1:26-27). As mentioned earlier, this *imago dei* (image of God) can't be thought of in physical terms. I hardly expect God to have the same physical, bodily form as a human being. But it is significant that we bear the impress of the divine. We are God's representatives on the earth, made to be treated with respect (Gen. 9:6). In human beings, we see something of the nature of God.

When we consider the nature of humanity—our pettiness, our hatred, our violence—it's difficult to believe that we could see God in each other. Surely lions are more majestic, eagles are more beautiful, and dogs are more loyal. Yet what species is so capable of love and compassion as our own? What creatures are so diverse, encompassing so many forms, features, and occupations? Which of the animals are so creative, which so enterprising? We are evil and fallen, to be sure, but what creature of earth comes closer to godhood than we? As the Spirit works in our lives, the divine image becomes even more apparent. As John writes, "How great is the love the Father has lavished on us, that we should be called children of God! *And that is what we are!*" (1 John 3:1, emphasis added).

It's not so incomprehensible, then, that in the Old Testament, God does us the honor of appearing in human form. Nor is it inconceivable that God does us the greater honor of becoming human in Jesus Christ. Through Christ, we see the perfect image of God, reflected in human form (Col. 2:9). In him, we see the Father (John 14:9). So if we would seek to know God better, perhaps we should look to the images that God himself has provided—in Jesus Christ, the saints of the church, and our brothers and sisters. If we would seek to serve God, we may do so by serving the representatives he has given all around us. In Jesus' lesson about the final judgment, he tells us that if we have served the least of his brothers and sisters, we have served the Lord (Matt. 25:31–46).

STATING THE PRINCIPLE

What is the principle behind the second commandment? Not that we don't have images of God. Images are necessary if we're to relate to God at all. Indeed, God himself supplied images when he appeared in human form to the prophets, and when he became incarnate in Jesus Christ. Rather, at issue is the character of our images. The Lord forbids human beings from creating images of God that are graven in stone or cast in metal—images that not only embody our own ideas but also are set and inflexible. Such images cannot begin to do justice to his glory and majesty.

If we must have images, perhaps it's best if they are the human images that God created. And let them be multiplied so that they embody many aspects of God's nature. Let our image of God include an inventor's creativity, a comedian's wit, a caretaker's compassion. But let's not cling to our images too tightly. Even the best images fall far short of God's transcendent nature. In the process of our Christian growth, God will be constantly shattering our images, replacing them with new and better ones, until the time when our liberated and glorified spirits can see him as he truly is.

QUESTIONS FOR REFLECTION

1. What are your favorite biblical images of God? How do these images help you relate to the Lord?
2. Do you have any personal images of God that aren't inspired by the Bible? Do you think they are a help or a hinderence to your Christian growth?
3. Have you ever prayed to an icon? Do you think icons are good for everyone, good for some people, or good for nobody?
4. What do you think of the idea that human beings reflect the nature of God? Who is the most godly person you know? What

makes him or her godly? Do you think the image of God dwelt in Adolph Hitler?

5. Read Matthew 25:31–46. How do people represent God? What is the relationship between worshiping God and serving other people?

f i v e

The Sanctity of God's Name

You shall not utter the name of the LORD your God falsely, for the
LORD will not excuse anyone who utters his name falsely.
—Exodus 20:7, author's translation

SOME TIME AGO, the newsmagazine show *20/20* did a story on the rising use of profanity by children. The cameras followed a potty-mouthed five-year-old at play, spewing out curse words like a sailor. The parents expressed concern about their child's language and mildly corrected him, but it was also obvious that they found his vocabulary entertaining. The cameras also visited a high school and recorded conversations between teenagers in the hallways. Every few words, the vilest epithets in the English language were casually thrown into the mix.

After the clip was over, hostess Barbara Walters asked the reporter who had covered the story what he felt should be done about the problem. He replied, "I don't see any big deal here. After all, it's only words."

Only words! What a strange comment coming from a journalist. If anyone should recognize the awesome power of words, it would be someone who makes a living with words—writing stories, carefully choosing each phrase, editing and re-editing. But this journalist's attitude is not uncommon. Many people have the notion that words are inconsequential. We've become so familiar with insults and obscenities that we've become desensitized to them. And yet how deeply can unkind words scar children or other sensitive souls.

Consider the story of Aleister Crowley. Crowley is regarded as the father of modern Satanism. During his lifetime, he proudly wore the title, "The Wickedest Man Alive." Though raised in a supposedly Christian home, his mother was a cruel, disturbed woman who would often beat young Crowley. The most formative event in his life occurred when he was about eight years old. He'd been disobedient to his mother, and she became livid. She screamed at him, "You're a devil! You're just plain evil. You know that beast in the book of Revelation? That's who you are!" Little Crowley decided that if he was the Beast, he might as well act like it. He began at that young age to investigate occultism, cruelty, and perversions. It wasn't so much the beatings that made him turn bad; rather, it was the cruel words that undercut his very personhood.

Clearly, words do make a difference. The person who said, "Sticks and stones can break my bones, but names can never hurt me," was probably never called names when he or she was a child. The names we give to people can be the most critical communication of all.

THE SIGNIFICANCE OF NAMES

Of course, most of us are aware that names can affect the way people perceive us. Hollywood is awash with people who have dumped a name that sounded too ethnic or average in favor of something more exotic, sexy, or masculine. A recent study asked subjects whom they'd choose for president of the United States, the vote based solely on the candidates' names. The vast majority chose Anglo-sounding names over different ethnic ones. Short names were preferred to longer names. The runaway favorites were names ending with an "-on" sound, like "Washington" or "Clinton." Even in our modern, enlightened times, we tend to associate the sound of a name with the ability to perform a job.

Our appreciation for names, however, pales in comparison to the significance that ancient peoples attached to them. For the people of biblical times, names were a window to the soul. As in our own day, parents chose names that reflected their hopes for their child or for a characteristic that they wanted to see the child develop. Such names were considered more than just hopeful; they were often regarded as prophetic. For example, Noah's name means "rest," and it's derived from his father's hope that Noah would give the world rest from the curse brought by Adam and Eve (Gen. 5:29). Samson's name comes from the Hebrew word for "sun," and it presages the child's illustrious future. Saul, first king of Israel, was named "requested"—probably meaning that his parents had asked for a son, but also auguring the way that the Israelites had requested a king and had gotten Saul. Many names in ancient times employed the name of God. The name Joshua means "the Lord saves" and hints at his prominent role in delivering Israel in the conquest of Canaan. Elijah's name means "my God is the Lord," and he certainly lives up to it in his struggle against the worship of the god Baal in Israel.

The sounds of names, too, were often considered to be significant. Moses' name sounds like the Hebrew word for "drawn" and was associated with the fact that he was drawn out of water by Pharaoh's daughter (Exod. 2:10). In fact, his name comes from an Egyptian word meaning "begotten," as in the Egyptian pharaoh names Thutmosis ("begotten of the god Thut") and Ramses ("begotten of Ra"). Jacob's name comes from a verb meaning "to supplant," but it sounds like the noun meaning "heel." So Jacob's name was connected with the story of how he was born clinging to Esau's heel (Gen. 25:26). In 1 Samuel 25, Nabal had the misfortune of inheriting a name that sounded like the Hebrew word for "fool." It's possible that he was named for a similar-sounding musical instrument or for a different homonym. In any event, the name "Nabal" represents a biblical sour note. According to the story, David had come to Nabal seeking some food for his soldiers, but Nabal rebuffed him. David armed his men to march against Nabal, but Nabal's wife, Abigail, dissuaded him, explaining, "May my lord pay no attention to that wicked man Nabal. He is just like his name—his name is Fool, and folly goes with him" (25:25).

It's also possible that Nabal was deliberately named "fool." In those days, parents believed that you could lure evil spirits if you gave your child a name that seemed to anticipate success or desirability.

Uncomplimentary names are not at all uncommon in ancient records. A child could end up with the name "ugly" because her parents were afraid that they'd be tempting fate if they named her "beautiful."

Other factors also were considered in choosing a name for a child. There were in those days, as in our day, family names that were passed down through generations. Ancient heroes' names were often chosen. The prophets Isaiah (Isa. 8:1-4) and Hosea (Hos. 1) gave their children symbolic names. Sometimes people picked names for their children just because they sounded good. But the biblical authors usually saw some significance in the names of great people.

In fact, when people entered into a new relationship or new phase of their lives, they often received new names to reflect their change in status. When Pharaoh Neco of Egypt conquered Judah, he placed King Josiah's son Eliakim ("God Has Lifted Up") on Judah's throne, but changed his name to Jehoiakim ("The Lord Has Lifted Up"; see 2 Kings 23:34). Not a significant difference of meaning, but a significant act, nonetheless. When Nebuchadnezzar of Babylon later conquered Judah, he installed Jehoiakim's brother Mattaniah ("Gift of the Lord") as king, changing his name to Zedekiah ("The Lord Is Righteous"; see 2 Kings 24:17). Through these name changes, the foreign kings were exercising their ultimate sovereignty over the Jewish underlings—they could even undo what their parents had done.

The Lord himself changed the names of Abram ("Great Father") to Abraham (same meaning, but similar in sound to the Hebrew word *hamon*, "multitude"; Gen. 17:5); Sarai (archaic Hebrew meaning "Princess") to Sarah (newer Hebrew meaning "Princess"; Gen. 17:15); and Jacob ("Supplanter") to Israel ("God Contends"; Gen. 32:28). These changes demonstrate that God considers names to be more than merely a convenient handle. Ideally, the name should reveal something of its bearer. When a person invokes a name, that person enters into a relationship with its bearer. And when God chooses someone's name, it's clear that the relationship is very significant, indeed. It's no wonder that the book of Revelation records that all who overcome in this world will receive a special name from God, known only to God and to the saint who receives it (Rev. 2:17).

THE NAME OF THE LORD

The name of the Lord, then, is especially significant. No one gave God his name—he chose it himself. It's part of the way in which God reveals his nature to us. It deserves a few moments of our attention to consider its meaning.

The most important names of God in the Old Testament are *El*, *Elohim*, and *Yahweh*. *El* basically means "mighty one," a term that brings to mind God's great power. *Elohim*, usually translated "God" in the Bible, really isn't a name at all—it's a noun that means both "God" and "gods." Nonetheless, in the Bible this word is frequently used like a proper name. Probably it's a plural form of the word from which the name *El* is derived, and it shares the basic meaning of "mighty one."

The reason for the plural form has been explained several ways. Some scholars argue that it derives from a time when the Israelites were polytheists, worshiping many gods instead of one. Others have argued that it's a "plural of majesty." Sometimes in the Hebrew language, when something is viewed as being particularly great or taken to its greatest extent, a plural noun is used. *Gevuroth*, for example, literally translates "strengths," and simply means "great strength." *'Adanim*, "pleasures," signifies "extreme delight." Thus, *elohim* could mean "the greatest God." (A similar phenomenon occurs in English, where the British monarchs refer to themselves with the royal "we.") Finally, the plural is often used to denote collective nouns—things that are more than one taken together as a single unit, as in our phrase "a pair of *pants*." Of course, Christians through the ages have argued that the use of a plural word to mean "God" is a reflection of God's trinitarian nature. Since God is three in one, the noun for God must also be plural. The main difficulty with this interpretation is that orthodox Christians maintain that God *isn't* a plurality. He really is just one God, though in three persons.

The most significant name of God, however, is the name *Yahweh* (usually translated "the LORD"). "Yahweh" is found in the book of Genesis as one of the names that the patriarchs used for their God. But the importance of the name wasn't really noted until the book of

Exodus, where Moses had a conversation with God about his name. When God first introduced himself to Moses, he identified himself merely as the God of Moses' ancestors—Abraham, Isaac, and Jacob (Exod. 3:6). To Moses, this wasn't good enough. He wanted to know God's name. Given the importance of names to these ancient peoples, Moses' interest is understandable. Perhaps by learning God's name, he could learn something more about God's nature. But God's immediate reply was merely, "I AM WHO I AM. This is what you are to say to the Israelites: 'I AM has sent me to you'" (Exod. 3:14).

It's safe to assume that "I AM" was not intended to be taken as God's name. Rather, the statement reveals something about God's nature, while at the same time concealing his nature. If God had said, "My name is Dagan [Hebrew for "grain"]," Moses would have known that God was an agricultural deity. If he'd said, "My name is Shemesh [Hebrew for "sun"]," Moses would have considered God a solar deity. But God wouldn't allow himself to be categorized in such a way. His most significant characteristic is his own existence; to label him further is futile and demeaning.

God, however, wasn't finished. He then told Moses that he was *YHWH*—God of Abraham, Isaac, and Jacob (Exod. 3:15). Moses at least heard something that really sounded like a name and not just a title. It appears that after making his point with the words, "I AM," God felt it was reasonable to tell the Israelites a name, so they could call on him properly. It was a special, significant act of self-revelation. God allowed himself to be known by his people. In a sense, he made himself vulnerable to them. Because once they knew his name, they had the power to misuse it.

The meaning of the name *YHWH*, and even its pronunciation, is somewhat in doubt. In ancient times, the Hebrew language was written with consonants only. Vowels were considered unnecessary, since texts were usually memorized anyway. It wasn't until the Middle Ages that signs representing the vowels were added. Jewish tradition had forbidden pronouncing the holy name of God many centuries earlier, thinking that the very act of pronouncing the name of God was to take it in vain (we'll discuss this idea later). Because of disuse the actual pronunciation of *YHWH* was forgotten. Instead, when the letters *YHWH* appeared in the text, the Jews would read *"adonai"* (Lord). Since we don't know the original pronunciation, we don't know if God told Moses that his name was *Yehweh,* "He Exists," or *Yahweh,* "He Causes to Be." Most scholars, however, prefer the latter pronunciation, relating the name to God's unique role as the Creator of heaven and Earth.

Other "names" of God in the Bible are actually just expansions on the names mentioned above. The name *Yahweh Sabaoth,* or "Lord of Hosts," adds the idea that God is in command of angelic legions. The name *El Shaddai* (Gen. 17:1; 28:3; etc.), often translated "God Almighty," probably means "God of the Hills." It alludes to God's preference for appearing on hills or mountaintops. Some other so-called names of God are actually place names and are not properly names of God at all. For example, *Yahweh Yireh* ("Jehovah Jireh"), meaning "The Lord Provides," is the name of the site where God provided a sacrifice in place of Isaac (Gen. 22:14).

The most significant names of God, then, were *El, Elohim,* and *Yahweh*—but *Yahweh* was the most important of all. To the biblical people, this name was a special window into God's nature. Indeed, "the Name," as it was known, came to be viewed almost as an extension of God's being. In many Bible verses, the phrase "the name of the Lord," or even "the Name," is used in place of saying "the Lord." For example, the books of 1 Kings and 2 Chronicles speak about Solomon building a temple for "the name of the Lord" (1 Kings 3:2; 5:3; 2 Chron. 2:1; 2:4; 6:7; etc.). Obviously, that's just another way of saying that he built a temple for the Lord. In Isaiah 59:19, the prophet writes that God will bring judgment on the nations in order that they might "fear the name of Yahweh" (see also Ps. 102:15). It's possible that someone could actually be afraid of God's name, but more likely it's God himself whom they would fear. The Psalms frequently enjoin us to "praise the name of Yahweh" (Pss. 7:17; 68:4; 113:1). Again, the phrase "the name of the Lord" simply means "the Lord." In Psalm 20:1 we read, "May the LORD answer you when you are in distress; may the name of the God of Jacob protect you." Here, the poetic structure of the psalm requires that "the name" and "the Lord" are synonyms. Such usage of the phrase "the Name" was so significant that by Jesus' time, "the Name" was one of the most important words used by the rabbis when they referred to God. Instead of saying, "When God delivered Israel from Egypt . . .", for example, the rabbis might say, "When the Name delivered Israel from Egypt . . ."

UTTERING GOD'S NAME FALSELY

Now that we understand what the Bible meant by God's name, let's turn our attention to the phrase, "take in vain." The verb "take," *nasa'*, in this verse literally means to pick up something or carry something away. When "take" refers to words, it means to speak or utter. The same phrase is used in Psalm 16:4, where the psalmist writes, "I will not . . . take up [the idolaters'] names on my lips." In context, it appears that the psalmist says that he won't bless them or wish them well.

The difficult word in the third commandment is *shawe*, usually translated "in vain." This word has a basic meaning of something that's empty or useless. *Shawe* is used in the Psalms to describe the ineffective aid of human beings, as opposed to God's powerful deliverance (Pss. 60:11; 108:12). Jeremiah describes Israel's idols with this same word, meaning that they're unable to provide any real help (Jer. 18:15). God describes the Israelites' sacrifices with this word, calling them "useless offerings," because the people gave offerings without repenting of their sins (Isa. 1:13). When the word *shawe* is used of speech, it usually means deception—an empty or false communication, because there's no truth behind it (see Ps. 144:8, 11; Prov. 30:8). The words of deceitful people are described as *shawe* in Psalm 26:4 and Job 11:11.

So the third commandment, "You shall not take the name of the Lord your God in vain," could be better translated, "You shall not utter God's name falsely"—which, unfortunately, doesn't make much sense. How do you utter a name falsely? A name isn't a statement with truth or untruth. Yet it's certainly possible to use a name under false pretenses or with false intentions. It may be, then, that the third commandment has in mind the misappropriation of God's name for deceptive purposes.

Recall the great significance that ancient peoples attached to names; a name was essentially an extension of a person's character. In this light, slander or character assassination might well be regarded as uttering a name falsely. Even today, we say that a malicious slanderer has ruined someone's "good name." What we mean, of course, is that his or her reputation has been sullied.

Let's consider now some biblical examples of violating the third commandment. Looking at these examples may help us to understand the principle behind the prohibition.

THE THIRD COMMANDMENT AND BLASPHEMY

The most egregious way that the third commandment could be violated was by blaspheming the Lord. Psalm 139:20 pleads for God to remove the evil men who "speak against you wickedly. They utter your name falsely" (author's translation). Here, the very words of the third commandment are identified with the slander of God. The book of Leviticus tells the story of a half-Egyptian man who got into a fight with an Israelite. In his anger, he blasphemed the name of the Lord with a curse. Because of his impiety, the man was stoned to death (Lev. 24:10–23).

Today, a charge of blasphemy is viewed with skepticism. Movie images of wild-eyed clerics pointing a bony finger and shrieking "Blasphemy!" have done an effective job of prejudicing us against charging someone with this particular sin. We may think of Galileo, accused of blasphemy because he argued that the earth revolves around the sun. Others may be reminded of the Spanish Inquisition, where Jews and Muslims—or anyone suspected of being a Jew or Muslim—met horrible deaths under the charge of blasphemy. The impression we get from movies and history books is that only religious fanatics are concerned about blasphemy. Modern-thinking individuals, we believe, aren't afraid of things that people might say about God.

The Bible, however, takes blasphemy very seriously, as it does any sin. In the Bible, blasphemy refers to anything said that attributes evil to God or that deliberately mocks him. Blasphemy is a sin of the impure use of our tongues—a direct insult to God. Blasphemy is not a matter of questioning God or even challenging God's will—many great saints in the Bible and throughout history have questioned God's will. A parent, grieving over the loss of a child, who hurls angry words at God has probably not committed blasphemy. Nor has the scientist whose studies may seem to some to undermine the teachings of the Bible or challenge widely held religious beliefs. Blasphemy must be a deliberate, public slander of God.

The fact that the words of the half-Egyptian blasphemer in Leviticus fall within this definition of blasphemy doesn't make us any more comfortable with the outcome. An angry man uttered some ignorant words. And for those hasty words, he paid with his life. Is this fair? If we read a news account about a woman who killed a man simply because he'd insulted her, we'd likely think the killer was a monster who should be locked away. We teach our children to ignore someone who calls them names—yet the Bible tells us that God kills a man who insults him!

Stories like these can cause honest doubts in sincere seekers. But we must realize that more is at stake, however, than simply God's ego. Blasphemy affects the whole community. When words are uttered that impugn God's character, everyone who hears them is victimized. Consider the context of the Leviticus incident. The Israelites had several times rebelled against Moses and God. They'd become discouraged and lamented that God had brought them out of Egypt simply to abandon them in the wilderness. They needed no one to stir up their doubts. The public blasphemy of God threatened to undermine the community. And in biblical economics, the life of one individual is far less significant than the souls of the entire community.

Modern society embraces some values that make it difficult for us to appreciate this principle. One such value is individualism. In America today, we tend to idolize the "cowboy spirit," the lone ranger who stands apart from the crowd. Every person has the right to "life, liberty, and the pursuit of happiness"—however he or she might conceive of that happiness. We have a hard time putting the needs of the community above the interests or emotions of an individual.

Another value is materialism. A living, breathing person seems intrinsically more valuable to us than an invisible, eternal soul. The idea of killing someone, or letting someone die, so that souls might be saved is abhorrent to us. We are shocked when members of the Jehovah's Witnesses allow their children to die rather than permit them to have blood transfusions. Yet they value the eternal welfare of their children more than their temporal, physical welfare.

Yet another value that gives us pause when we read the story in Leviticus is our passion for free speech. We think that everyone should have the right to express his or her opinion, even if that opinion threatens the stability of our society. Neo-Nazis and Ku Klux Klan members are permitted to declare their lunacy on podiums in African-American neighborhoods; public libraries are allowed to display pornography; protesters are allowed to burn flags during wartime because we cherish freedom of speech so highly. Also, we tend to idealize the rebel, the person who stands against the status quo. We like to cheer for the underdog, even if that person is clearly in the wrong.

A final value is what one of my seminary professors called "compassion run amok." We want to be gentle, forgiving people, accepting of everyone and everything. Yet if we really allowed everyone to live by these ideals, our society would come apart at the seams. It would be impossible for us to cooperate for the public good if everyone's individual "good" were given higher priority.

Today, blasphemy isn't a topic of serious discussion. Perhaps, because we no longer live in communities bound together by religious beliefs, blasphemy doesn't have the same social repercussions that it had in ancient days. But the good of the community is only secondarily at stake—the real concern is the honor of God's good name.

THE THIRD COMMANDMENT AND OATHS

In ancient times, a very important application of the third commandment concerned the use of God's name in oaths. When someone took a vow, or when two parties joined into an agreement with one another, they'd call upon a deity to act as a witness—sort of a divine notary public. Often, the vow was accompanied by some kind of symbolic gesture, like the slaughter of an animal or the breaking of a pot. The person taking the vow would say, "May the Lord do so to me, and more also, if I do not fulfill my vow!" In other words, they called on God to punish them severely if they failed to do what they said they'd do.

What if someone had taken such a vow but had no intention of fulfilling it? According to the Bible, they had taken the name of the Lord in vain. Psalm 24:4, for instance, identifies "he whose soul utters falsely" (a clear reference to violating the third commandment) with "he who swears deceitfully" (author's translation). Leviticus 19:12 alludes to the third commandment when it says, "Do not swear falsely by my name and so profane the name of your God." When Jesus said, "You have heard that it was said to the people long ago, 'Do not break your oath, but keep the oaths you have made to the Lord'" (Matt. 5:33), he, as well, likely had in mind the third commandment, considering that the remark occurs in the midst of an exposition on the Ten Commandments. Also, by Jesus' time, it's clear that the Jewish rabbis primarily identified violating the third commandment with breaking oaths. The old Aramaic translations of the Old Testament, made around the time of Jesus, render the third commandment, "You shall not swear falsely by the name of the Lord your God." The same interpretation can be found in old rabbinic literature, dating from the first four centuries A.D.

The connotation associated with "swear falsely" remains in our modern "vocabulary of obscenity." When people use off-color words, we say that they're "swearing." In the old days, they'd have said that they "uttered an oath." We talk about foul language as "profanity"—language that shows contempt for that which is sacred. Undoubtedly, of the many words used by people when they strike their thumb with a hammer or when they're frustrated about their taxes, "God" and "Jesus Christ" still come near the top of the list. They're not invoking God's name in prayer. They are taking God's name in vain, uttering empty "oaths," without even realizing the significance of the exclamation.

In biblical times, empty vows demonstrated a lack of respect for God's power. The person who made an oath called on God to witness the vow, even dared God to kill him or her if the vow was broken. But the oath-maker didn't really expect God to follow through. An attitude of superiority may have been involved. The oath-breaker had the power to use God (or at least God's name) for his of her own purposes, but believed that God couldn't do anything to him or her in return.

In modern times, most people who casually invoke God's name don't do so with the idea of taking a vow. Sometimes you'll hear something like, "I swear to God, I'll stand behind you when you talk to the boss!" If your coworker says this with no intention of following through, the situation is much the same as with oath-breakers in biblical times. She believes that God is unable to hold her accountable for what she swore to do, and demonstrates contempt for God's power. Regardless if a person makes a vow sincerely, Jesus warned that it's best not to take such oaths (Matt. 5:33–37). He instructed that if you intend to do something, you don't need to take a vow—just do it! For people of true integrity, oaths are unnecessary.

While people who swear a false oath show disregard for God, people who use God's name as a curse word are just being thoughtless. They aren't thinking about God at all as his name gushes out of their lips. For the most part, potty-mouthed people intend no disrespect. There's no intent to deceive, no malice against God. Usually, their use of profanity is no more than a habit. The average Joe has probably never considered how he'd feel if his daughter, every time she became irritated, contemptuously uttered Joe's name under her breath. If the thoughtless use of such language shows a lack of respect for God, it's because our society—more than the individuals in it—has become disrespectful. The attitudes of society, however, don't excuse the individual, and it's a sad commentary on society when disrespect for God has become a cultural norm. The individuals may be innocent of serious sin, but they reflect and perpetuate the nonchalance toward God that is typical of our time.

Still others might get a thrill from speaking God's name contemptuously, daring God to do something about it. I'm reminded of the story of John Newton, the great writer who gave us the hymn, "Amazing Grace." Before his conversion, he would sometimes make up very different kinds of songs—ditties designed to mock God and those who believed in him. Such mockers aren't breaking a vow—they're committing blasphemy. In an earlier time, they would have paid with their lives. Nowadays, it's only their souls they have to worry about.

AVOIDING ALL UTTERANCES

By Jesus' time, the Jews had developed a radical way of obeying the third commandment. They wouldn't say God's name at all. An almost superstitious awe was attached to the name of the Lord, so that his name, *Yahweh,* was never pronounced aloud. When Scripture was read in the synagogues, the readers would say *Adonai,* "Lord," instead of the name *Yahweh.* When the biblical text was copied by scribes, they would often write the Divine Name in archaic script letters instead of contemporary forms, or they would replace the letters with dots: • • • •. They didn't even want to write the Name, for fear of violating the third commandment.

The practice of avoiding the pronunciation of God's name gave us the name "Jehovah." Recall that Hebrew was originally written without vowels, its alphabet consisting entirely of consonants. In the Middle Ages, Jewish scribes invented a system of vowel signs to make the Hebrew Bible easier to read. At that time two major Hebrew Bible traditions were already in existence—the written text, copied by the scribes of each generation, and the oral text, carefully memorized and passed on through the ages by recitation. When the scribes added the vowels to the text, they used the oral text as their guide to pronunciation. Sometimes, the oral text and the written text differed. In such cases, the scribes often made a note in the margin, but went ahead and wrote down the vowels of the word they pronounced. Since the Jews would say *"Adonai"* wherever the written text said *"YHWH,"* the scribes placed the vowels for *Adonai* among the consonants for *YHWH,* resulting in YeHoWaH—which we pronounce "Jehovah."

Originally, the practice of not writing or speaking the name of God may have arisen from simple superstition. An ancient belief existed that uttering the name of a spirit could cause that spirit to appear. Recall again the significance attached to names in those times. Names reflected the essence of persons or spirits and so could be used to gain a measure of control over them. A principle of magic was that "names of power" could be used to gain mastery over demons— thus the source of our saying, "Speak of the Devil!" If you speak about the Devil, he's bound to put in an appearance. Likewise, ancient people believed that if you uttered God's name, you might inadvertently summon God. However much the ancient Jews loved the Lord, they didn't want to summon him unnecessarily! Thus, they believed that it was best not to speak God's name aloud unless you really meant it. From the avoidance of *casual* mention of God's name came a more general avoidance of *any* mention of God's name. In fact, some modern Orthodox Jews won't even say or write the word "God." Instead, they write G-d.

We might smirk at this hypercorrect behavior, but there's a healthy dose of respect behind it. It reflects an understanding that God is fearful and awesome—not a God we carry around in our coat pocket. Popular Christian music and preaching sometimes depict God as a cosmic teddy bear, all warm and cuddly. Love is his most prominent quality, and all else—including his holiness—is relegated to second place. Sometimes God is treated like a domestic servant, at our every beck and call. His job is to make us healthy, wealthy, and happy. That, however, is not the God of the Bible. In the Scriptures, God is fearsome. There's a sense of frightening unpredictability to God that even his most devoted worshipers must acknowledge. God challenged Abraham to sacrifice his only son. God almost killed Moses because he hadn't circumcised his son. He caused Ezekiel to wander about naked. And let's not even mention what God allowed to happen to poor Job. It's no wonder that when Isaiah saw the Lord, he was terrified, and said, "Woe to me! I am ruined!" (Isa. 6:5). The Bible tells us that the fear of the Lord is the beginning of wisdom—not a cowering, cringing fear of mistrust and ignorance, but a healthy respect for one whose power and purposes are unfathomable to our limited minds. We must recognize that while God has only our good in mind, the comfort—or even the life—of any individual is a small thing in view of God's eternal plan.

THE PRINCIPLE OF RESPECT

Undoubtedly, the principle behind the third commandment is one of respect for God. We aren't to slander God's character, to use his name in vows that we don't intend to keep, or even to bandy his name about casually. To do so reveals a lack of belief in God's power, in

God's holiness, or in both. The name of God reflects the character of God and should be treated with the respect that we would show God himself.

Not many of us are tempted these days to make a false vow in God's name. Most Christians, too, avoid swearing, at least with God's name. Yet we may well be accused of having become a little too familiar with God. I'm still disturbed by children who call their parents by their first names. There is benefit in observing the formality of titles. They remind children that there's a necessary imbalance to the parent-child relationship. Wisdom, power, and authority belong to the parent, and they must be given due respect. If children don't have the proper respect for their parents, the children will suffer from maladjustment and mistrust. They might even injure themselves, ignoring the parents' warnings about crossing the street or playing with matches.

While we do enjoy intimacy with our God, it's wise to remember who we are and who God is. Our relationship with God is not one between equals. Wisdom, power, and authority are God's. If we don't show God the respect that's his due, we won't hurt him, but we could harm ourselves. We do well to give serious thought to the way we talk about God. The words we speak make a difference in the way we think—about God and about ourselves.

QUESTIONS FOR REFLECTION

1. How have words spoken to you affected your self-image, for good or for bad?
2. Do you think your name reflects your personality? If you could choose any name for yourself, what would it be?
3. Why is it important for God to have a name? Could we relate as easily to a nameless deity?
4. Do you think you'd feel more respect for God if you avoided uttering his name?
5. Do you think Christians have become too "familiar" with God? Why or why not?

s i x

The Rest of Your Week

*Remember the Sabbath day by keeping it holy. Six days you shall labor
and do all your work, but the seventh day is a Sabbath to the* LORD
*your God. On it you shall not do any work, neither you, nor your
son or daughter, nor your manservant or maidservant, nor
your animals, nor the alien within your gates. For in six days
the* LORD *made the heavens and the earth, the sea, and all that
is in them, but he rested on the seventh day. Therefore the*
LORD *blessed the Sabbath day and made it holy.*
—Exodus 20:8-11

THE FOURTH COMMANDMENT DEPARTS from the pattern set by the first
three. First, it has a different form. The first three were all worded as
prohibitions: "You shall not have other gods. . . ." "You shall not make
idols. . . ." "You shall not utter God's name falsely. . . ." The fourth
commandment, however, begins with a prescription: "You shall remember the Sabbath." The prohibitions follow. No doubt there's a significant
reason for this change. Prohibitions are restrictive and address a specific
behavior. Consider two statements: "Don't drive over fifty-five miles per
hour," and "Always drive under fifty-five miles per hour." They mean
essentially the same thing, but the prohibition speaks only about unacceptable behavior. It says nothing about how free we are to drive below
the limit. The prescription, however, gives us *permission* to drive under

fifty-five miles per hour. Even though the second statement technically means the same thing as the first, it's *literally* concerned with acceptable driving, not unacceptable driving. A different psychological dynamic is involved. Likewise, a prohibition, "Don't forget the Sabbath Day," would technically mean the same thing as the fourth commandment, but it would have a different psychological impact.

Why this change of form? Perhaps the commandment is deliberately worded to cast Sabbath-keeping in a positive light. Today, it's hard to explain the importance of keeping the Sabbath in terms of one's obligations to God. It's easy to see why God would want exclusive devotion, or why he would ask people to abstain from irreverently bandying about his name. But why should God be so concerned about work habits? Furthermore, it's very difficult to explain this commandment on the basis of some "situational ethic." Logical or ethical arguments could be raised as to why one shouldn't kill or steal, based on the universally recognized principle of "don't do to someone else what you wouldn't want them to do to you" (the so-called "Silver Rule," propounded by Buddha). But the benefits of not working on one day a week wouldn't be very apparent to ancient agricultural peoples. There were cows to milk, fields to sow. Would anyone really suffer if the shepherd sheared his sheep on a Saturday? Perhaps to overcome the natural psychological resistance to a day of rest, this commandment is formulated in more positive terms than the others.

This change in form is accompanied too by a change in subject matter. The first three commandments specifically address our relationship with God. We are commanded to have an exclusive relationship with God, to avoid constraining God to an image, and to treat God with due respect. The fourth commandment introduces a different idea. It's not solely concerned with our relationship to God, but also with our relationship to creation in general. The fourth commandment is perhaps the most comprehensive of the ten, because it touches on our relationship with God, our relationship with the earth, our relationship with each other, and our care for ourselves.

The Israelites probably would have been happy if the Lord had stopped with just three commandments. First, God regulated their worship practices, taking away their other gods and their idols. Now, God was telling them how to do their jobs! Some of them must have been thinking that this God of Sinai was a little too demanding. Yet the Lord wasn't just meddling. The Israelites expected God to provide them with food and safety. It seems reasonable that he had the right to dictate the circumstances under which these blessings would continue to flow.

Beginning with the fourth commandment, God demonstrates his concern with every area of our lives. He won't be confined to just the religious stuff. We can't discharge our full duty to God through mere observance of worship formalities. With the Sabbath day command, the commandments branched out into other areas of life. And number four is only the beginning; the commandments that follow become even more intrusive, regulating our human relations and even our thoughts—not one day, but every day of the week.

THE MEANING OF THE SABBATH

The phrase, "Remember the Sabbath day by keeping it holy," requires unpacking, beginning with the significant words. The verse begins with a commandment to "remember." Our idea of remembering is insipid compared to the Hebrew idea. When the Israelites were told to "remember the Exodus," they were in essence commanded to annually *relive* the event. According to Exodus 13:3 and Deuteronomy 16:3, they were to remember the Exodus by eating only unleavened bread, as their ancestors had eaten unleavened bread in their haste to leave Egypt. To remember the Exodus was to experience it anew. To remember the Sabbath was to experience it anew, as well. God had done no work on the original Sabbath, and the Israelites were to relive that day by doing no work.

The central feature of the Sabbath day was expressed in the very word "Sabbath." The word is an English form of the Hebrew word *shabbat,* meaning "ceasing" or "ending." When *shabbat* is applied to the Sabbath day, it had a dual significance. First, it meant the end of the week. "Sabbath" was the Hebrew name for Saturday, which of course is the last day of the week. (We'll talk about why Christians observe Sunday as the Sabbath below.) It also referred to the story of Creation, where God ceased *(shabbat)* his work on the seventh day (Gen. 2:2–3). We needn't be concerned about the question of whether or not God gets tired and needs to take a break. The Hebrew word *shabbat* doesn't necessarily imply that God was tired; it only means that he stopped the work he was doing. When God ceased from work on the seventh day, he established a pattern for the order of the world—work for a time, then a period of rest.

That's an important fact to note. The Sabbath day wasn't established after the fall of humanity. It's not part of the curses pronounced on Adam and Eve, curses that were partially revoked by Jesus Christ. Nor was the Sabbath day a "Jewish thing," like circumcision or the kosher laws, designed to set the Israelites apart from other nations. The Sabbath day is part of the order of Creation. That means that it remains in effect for as long as the world continues to exist.

The Sabbath, too, was to be holy. As explained in an earlier chapter, the word "holy" simply means "set apart for God." "Holiness" doesn't *necessarily* imply anything about one's morality or goodness. Obeying God's command to abstain from pork made the Israelites holy because it set them apart for God's sake from the nations around them (see Lev. 20:24–26). The Sabbath day was holy because it was set apart from the other days of the week as one in which people did no work. The Sabbath was also holy because it was "the Lord's day." So the Israelites kept the Sabbath not only as a day of leisure but also as a day of worship, study, and drawing close to God.

These, then, are the characteristics of the Sabbath day: It is to be a day when we cease work; it is a day when we worship. It seems a simple enough concept. Yet this fourth commandment is so easily disregarded.

PROBLEMS WITH OBSERVING THE SABBATH

The fourth commandment presents a dilemma in modern times. Life is fast-paced and continuous. New York isn't the only "city that never sleeps." We do our shopping on Sundays, which means someone has to work in the grocery stores. We travel, which means someone has to drive the bus, fly the plane, or take our money at the gas station. We have to pump the gas ourselves—isn't that doing work? We go to church, which means someone has to preach, or teach, or turn on the heat and lights in the building. In our modern world, how can anyone really stop working on the Sabbath day?

Thoughtful people sometimes have theological problems with the rationale behind the commandment. Does God really need to rest? But as explained previously, "rest" in this context only means to stop working. Rest doesn't suggest that God became tired, thus no contradiction exists with the doctrine of God's omnipotence. Many people would claim that God never stops working, but the idea in the fourth commandment is that God ceased the original work of *creation*. The world and all it contains have been established in their entirety; the physical laws have been fixed as constants. Even scientists would agree that the universe is complete and the laws of nature are fixed. The universe shall continue along its set course, and God doesn't need to undertake new acts of creation.

Other people have difficulty accepting the story of a literal seven-day creation week. Indeed, the first chapter of Genesis, the story of Creation, isn't presented in the narrative style of a history lesson. It's presented in the style of Hebrew poetry, with repetitive structure, phrases, and parallelisms. Based on this fact, some conclude that the story wasn't intended to be read as literal history, but rather as theological reflection. If the world wasn't created in a literal six days, however, the rationale behind the Sabbath rest is lost.

But even if the Creation story is a poetic and symbolic account of the universe's origins, that doesn't mean its lessons are not valid. Some of the most sublime truths in the Bible are expressed in symbolic or poetic language—the parables of Jesus, for example, or the triumph of God's people described in the book of Revelation. The lessons of the Creation account in Genesis 1-2:4 are clear: God is the Creator; Creation is gradual and systematic; and the work of Creation is, in some sense, complete. Although the universe is still changing, growing, and decaying, the laws of nature have been established as permanent statutes. One of those laws is that all created beings need both work and rest.

Another controversy regarding this commandment concerns the

definition of "rest" and "work." Well-meaning people might want to avoid breaking the Sabbath, but how can they do so if they don't know what constitutes work? This problem was debated even before the time of Jesus. We'll need to consider it in some detail.

DEFINING WORK

Physicists define work as a force acting over a distance. If you blasted a spaceship into orbit, into a hypothetical perfect vacuum of space, and then shut off its engines, the ship would continue to travel at its same velocity. It's not doing any work, however, because there's no force being applied to the ship. Or, a man could push against a building with all his might, trying to make the building fall over, but no work is done (except the work involved in the movement of his muscles). The building does not move, so all the force he exerts doesn't operate over a distance.

The physicists' definition of work is very helpful in engineering calculations, but it's not very helpful for those of us wrestling with the relevance of the fourth commandment in our everyday lives. According to the physicist, almost everything we do requires some measure of work. Any time that we exert even the least effort over space and time, we're working. In fact, we probably do more work when we play than we do when we work. We do work when we play a game of football. We exert energy over long and short distances, trying to move the ball to the end zone. We also do work, albeit to a lesser degree, when we eat our lunch, using force to move our sandwiches to our mouths. But many of us do very little work when we are actually *at* work, for instance poring over balance sheets or reading a professional paper.

Other people define work as the job that they get paid for doing. According to this definition, then, most homemakers do no work at all. People who live off the land, raise their own food, make their clothes, or barter for what they need don't work, either. Paid vacations, however, *are* work. Obviously, we need to rethink that definition!

The Bible doesn't say much about what constitutes work. The only Old Testament passage that even hints at what might be included is

Jeremiah 17:19–27. In these verses, the Lord, through the prophet, castigates the Jews for carrying loads and bringing goods in through the gates of Jerusalem on the Sabbath day. The principle was that the Jews weren't supposed to engage in commerce. But a literal-minded person would undoubtedly wonder, "All right then—how do you define a 'load'? Something that's a load for you may not be a load for me." Getting technical about Sabbath observance results in endless nit-picking.

The difficulties are illustrated well in the Jewish rabbis' attempts to define work. Like all points of law, the Jewish holy writings (the Mishnah and Talmud) contain various opinions on the matter. The rabbis debated long over issues of work. A principle that guided their debates was that work was not defined as a person's profession. Rather, work was defined by a certain level of physical exertion. So people could walk one thousand or two thousand feet from their homes, but they couldn't walk three thousand feet—that would be a violation of the Sabbath. It didn't matter that a walk of even a thousand feet could be a great exertion for an old rabbi, they had to settle on a definition. They decided that you could tie a knot on the Sabbath, but only if it could be tied with one hand. You could rearrange your pillow with your head, but you weren't allowed to fluff it with your hands. You couldn't write more than two letters at a time. You weren't permitted to trim your toenails. You couldn't set a broken bone. In fact, you weren't permitted to give any medical attention to someone, unless that person's life was in danger. It's no wonder that Jesus incurred the wrath of the Pharisees when he healed a man's hand on the Sabbath day.

JESUS ON THE SABBATH

Jesus' attitude toward keeping the Sabbath contrasts strongly with that of the rabbis. While they were concerned with defining work and abiding by the letter of the Law, Jesus was interested in upholding its spirit. The gospel of Mark begins its discussions of the Sabbath with an interesting story. Jesus and his disciples were passing through a field of grain on the Sabbath, and his disciples picked and ate the heads of grain. Such conduct was perfectly legal; farmers were commanded to allow people to glean from their fields. But the Pharisees criticized the disciples for "working" on the Sabbath. Jesus reminded the Pharisees of the story from the Old Testament in which David and his men ate consecrated bread in the temple. They were in need and used holy bread to fill that need. Citing this incident, Jesus implied that a respect for God's holiness shouldn't forbid people from fulfilling their human needs. He concluded, "The Sabbath is made for the sake of people; people aren't made for the sake of the Sabbath" (Mark 2:27, author's translation).

Jesus demonstrates this principle a number of times. On several occasions, he healed the sick on the Sabbath day. When the Pharisees challenged his actions, he asked, "If one of you has a son or an ox that falls into a well on the Sabbath day, will you not immediately pull him out?" (Luke 14:5). According to the rabbis' guidelines, the answer should be, "As long as the animal or person isn't in immediate danger, they should remain until the Sabbath is done." Jesus implies that, in actuality, no one would leave his animal or child in such a state. Sabbath or no Sabbath, he'd pull them out of the well.

Jesus' approach to Sabbath observance is marked by simple practicality. The Sabbath was created for *our* good, not God's good. It's supposed to be a day of rest and refreshment. If we keep the Sabbath in a way that becomes a burden, then its very purpose has been defeated. Resting shouldn't be a chore.

PRACTICALITY OF REST

Setting theological considerations aside for the moment, Jesus' approach to the Sabbath simply makes good sense. Our bodies—indeed, all physical things—need times of rest and recuperation. Recently, we've seen the effects of nonstop work on Japanese middle managers. The Japanese government has been alarmed by the number of young people who have died solely from exhaustion. History, too, has shown that a day of rest in seven is beneficial. During the French Revolution, an attempt was made to replace the seven-day week with a ten-day week. Voltaire reasoned, "To overthrow Christianity, we must overthrow the Christian Sabbath."

The experiment was a dismal failure, as people and even horses were collapsing under the new schedule. A day of rest among seven seems to be a very good system. It keeps us from overburdening ourselves and prevents the exploitation of employees or servants.

Practically speaking, too, rest means different things to different people. Perhaps the biggest problem with the rabbinic regulations were their "one-size-fits-all" work and rest pattern. They assume that each individual finds the same pursuits to be exerting and the same tasks to be exhausting. The rabbinic system didn't recognize that some people would find a stroll of a mile to be very relaxing and invigorating; some would find writing poetry to be restful; still others might be renewed by swinging a hammer or shopping at a mall. Some people might find the study of the holy books to be work! There can be no "one-size-fits-all" Sabbath. We all find our joy and rest in different ways.

Indeed, the Sabbath should be a day of joy. The book of Isaiah criticizes those who found the Sabbath to be a burden, who couldn't wait for it to be over so they could get back to doing their business and making transactions. Instead, the Sabbath should be a delight (Isa. 58:13). The rabbis took at least this verse to heart and recommended the Sabbath for sexual relations—apparently mindless of the exertion it could involve. Frequently though, among Christians, the idea of the Sabbath being a pleasurable day has been neglected. I read a story about a young pastor who skated to Sunday services over a frozen river because a snowstorm had blocked the roadways. The church elders were appalled that he would engage in recreation on the Sabbath, and they asked the minister to explain himself. He gave his rationale. One of the elders asked the minister if he had enjoyed the skate. When he answered that he had not, the elders deemed that his actions were acceptable.

What a sad parody of true Sabbath observance! God has no desire that we make ourselves miserable on the Sabbath. True, God may not be pleased with someone whose greatest joy is making money and who chooses to pursue it with zeal seven days a week. But neither does God desire that the Sabbath be made a day of gloom and doom. To do so is not compatible with the Sabbath being our day of corporate worship, since worship, above all, is to be a time of celebration.

REST AND WORSHIP

How did the ideas of a day of rest and a day of worship become combined? The roots of the practice come from Jewish observances. On the Sabbath day, the Israelites offered regular sacrifices to God as part of their worship practices (Num. 28:9–10). Oddly enough, the hard labor involved in bringing the animals to the temple, slaughtering them, hauling them up on to the altar, and so forth, was not considered a violation of the Sabbath regulation against work. Thus, it seems obvious that the Sabbath was never intended as an unrealistic avoidance of all physical exertion. Rather, it was meant to be a day of refreshment and renewal—and what could be more renewing than time worshiping in the presence of God, the giver of life? Later, the Jews continued the practice of Sabbath-day worship by meeting in synagogues on Saturday for prayer and to study the Scriptures.

For Christians, the Sabbath day was quickly displaced by "the Lord's day"—Sunday—as the day of worship. As early as New Testament times, it appears that Christians assembled on the first day of the week (Acts 20:7; 1 Cor. 16:2). Both theological and practical reasons accounted for this shift. First and foremost, Sunday was the day Jesus rose from the dead. Since the celebration of Christ's resurrection was the central focus of Christian worship, it was fitting to meet on the day he rose from the dead. Furthermore, it was argued, God created light on the first day, and Jesus is the Light of the World. It was even more fitting, then, that the celebration of Jesus would best take place on the first day of the week. Then, there was a practical consideration: Christianity had spread quickly in the Roman world among slaves. Slaves were required to work on Saturday, but on Sunday, the "day of the Sun," slaves could get away to worship. Thus we can see that the practicality characterizing Jesus' approach to the Sabbath characterized that of his followers as well.

The idea that Sunday would be officially a day of rest as well as worship originated somewhat later. It's possible that the early non-Jewish believers didn't emphasize the importance of a rest day because they saw it as a "Jewish thing." In fact, ancient pagan (non-Christian) writers often accused the Jews of laziness because they insisted on taking their day of rest each week. By the time of the Emperor Constantine, however, Sunday had become a day of *rest* for Christians as well as a day of worship. Constantine passed a decree in A.D. 321 suspending all business on Sundays. No one would then be compelled to work on the day preserved as a day of rest and worship.

Worship should be a pleasurable, life-affirming experience. It should be joyous and refreshing. If we find it a burdensome chore to attend church, there could be two causes. One, the services at your church might be boring, uninspired, or simply not fitting for *you,* in which case you should find another church. Two, perhaps you go to church with the wrong expectations. Too many people today attend church with the hope of being entertained. They want the church to lift their spirits and make them happy. Perhaps if more people came with the desire to do something for God, to worship him and to help others to worship, then church wouldn't seem so dry. We certainly don't violate the Sabbath by doing the work of lifting our voices in song, carrying the burden of a brother or sister, or exerting ourselves to experience God in the words of Scripture.

WHY A SABBATH DAY?

This, then, is the principle behind the Sabbath: It's a day of suspending our work in order to allow our bodies to recharge. It's also a day to set aside time for corporate worship, so that we can grow closer to our God, the source of life and peace.

Of course, we can rest any day of the week—some people seem to rest every day of the week. We can also worship every day, and indeed, we should. Is it really necessary to set aside a day for these activities? Why not rest for four hours a day for six days of the week? Why not worship ten minutes each day, instead of an hour on Sunday?

The Bible doesn't address these questions, but perhaps the answer is biological: circadian rhythm. Our bodies, and the bodies of all earthly creatures, are set to run on a twenty-four-hour cycle. We have an internal clock that regulates our periods of activity and inactivity. It's roughly tuned, of course, to the rising and setting of the sun, but even people who are deprived of sunlight for long periods continue on roughly a twenty-four-hour cycle. So as long as the world keeps turning at its current pace, the day is the most natural division of our week.

Our modern society does, indeed, move at a frantic, seven-day-a-week pace. It's easy to get caught up into its headlong rush. Our time is so jam-packed with activities that our lives can hardly contain them. We just have to make it to another meeting, make another phone call, watch another TV show. We work longer hours, then we stop off at the gym to work off the stress—as well as the fast food that is the staple of many American diets. We have board meetings in the evening; the kids have to get to music lessons and student council. We're going to an outing in the park on Tuesday, building a house with Habitat for Humanity on Saturday, and we have to squeeze in time to go to our support group meeting on Friday. Studies show that modern conveniences give Americans more leisure time than ever, but it's in smaller chunks than it used to be. We hardly put together two hours to rest, let alone a whole day. It's no wonder we're a nation in therapy.

Yet we Christians are called to reject the world's values. The materialism, greed, and freneticism that characterize many people today are in direct conflict with the value of simplicity recommended by Jesus Christ. How can we find peace when we're always pushing for something bigger and better? We dash from one appointment to another; fight to win the next promotion or, better yet, the next job that pays so much more; try to get our kids into the best universities. Haven't the examples of O. J. Simpson, Elvis Presley, and Ernest Hemingway taught us that money, talent, and accomplishments won't make us happy? Haven't we seen that some of the most famous people in the world are also the most miserable? Jesus never said the words, but they are clear in his spirit: 'Tis a gift to be simple. No trophies we can put on our shelves or accolades we can help our children acquire will ever replace the joy of simple peace and rest.

Yes, even our good activities can draw us away from resting with God. Many causes are looking for volunteers who can give an hour here or a couple of hours there to help change unjust practices or ease human suffering. We could devote every free hour to worthwhile pursuits and go to bed at night feeling like we have accomplished something substantial. But let's not forget the lesson of Mary and Martha

(Luke 10:38–42). Martha was busy with the important work of preparing dinner for the Lord, while Mary sat at the Lord's feet and learned from him. Martha complained to Jesus about Mary's indolence, but Jesus gently reminded her that very little of what we do is really *essential.* The big dinner wasn't essential—Jesus would have been happy with simpler fare and a chance to enjoy Martha's company.

There's always a good cause that will take all the time and energy that you're willing to give. Even church will fill your schedule with so many meetings and events that you never have time to really know the Lord. God commands us to rest, to refresh ourselves, and to enjoy his presence. He invites us to come away with him, to share his company. Perhaps he'll meet you in the pages of a good novel, by the side of a river, or on a long afternoon walk. Perhaps you'll find refreshment and peace in a picnic at the park. Remember, there's no "one-size-fits-all" Sabbath. All God asks is that you break away from your work routine, and spend one day a week in activities that energize you and draw you close to God.

One day a week set apart for God. His fourth commandment is not a mean-spirited, petty demand. It could be the key to spiritual growth that you've been searching for.

QUESTIONS FOR REFLECTION

1. Do you have different feelings about the "positive commandments" than the negative ones? Which do you prefer?
2. How was the Sabbath observed in your home when you were a child?
3. Do you think that we are busier now than we used to be? How is this a good thing? How is it a bad thing?
4. Why do you think the rabbis developed so many rules about keeping the Sabbath? How might such rules be helpful?
5. What activities do you find most refreshing and rewarding? Do you think that they draw you closer to God? *Could* they draw you closer to God if you did them differently?

s e v e n

God's Perspective on Parents

Honor your father and your mother, so that you may live long in the land the LORD your God is giving you.
—Exodus 20:12

THE FIFTH COMMANDMENT IS often considered a bridge across the commandments. The first three commandments, and to a lesser extent the fourth, deal primarily with our obligation to God—the proper way to worship God and how to please him. The last five deal with our relationships with other human beings—how we get along with one another. Parents are human beings, of course, so this commandment seems to belong with the last five. But as we'll see, the fifth commandment also has much in common with the first four. Having connections with both halves of the Ten Commandments, the fifth commandment binds our obligations to God together with our obligations to others.

Let's consider the similarities between the fifth commandment and the first four. First, there is similar vocabulary. The first four commandments all use the phrase, "The LORD *(Yahweh)* your God." That's an appropriate phrase in commandments dealing with Israel's obligations to God, the God with whom they had an exclusive relationship. The last five commandments—in which the Lord's sovereignty isn't at issue—don't use the phrase. But the fifth commandment, which seems to be concerned with *human* relationships, uses this very phrase almost as if it was tacked on at the end. The meaning of the text wouldn't be substantially altered if the phrase weren't there. Yet this phrase links the language of the fifth commandment with that of the preceding commandments, reminding us that, though the subject matter has changed, the entire corpus of the Ten Commandments is concerned with defining what it means to be God's people.

This little phrase isn't the only connection between the fifth commandment and the first four. A more substantial link is that of subject matter. The relationship between parents and children is the most fundamental of all human relationships. It's the first relationship we experience, the one that defines us more fully than any other. It's second in significance only to our relationship with God, and in some ways it mirrors our relationship with God.

Just as God is the source of all life, our parents are the instruments that God uses to give us life. God provides all the necessities of life for every creature of earth (Ps. 145:15–16). While we're in the womb, our mother sustains us with her own blood, her own air, her own food. After we're born, our parents continue to provide for us until we're old enough to fend for ourselves. God protects us from harm, but when we're children, that role belongs to the parents, as well. God is our moral guide and our authority. He teaches us his values and corrects us when we err. Likewise, good parents seek to impart their own values to their children, and they'll discipline them when necessary to keep them on the path. It's no wonder that the Bible speaks of God as our Father and occasionally compares God to our mother as well (see Isa. 66:13).

Since our relationship with our parents is the closest thing on earth to our relationship with God, the fifth commandment uses some lofty-sounding language. The word "honor" means that we're to grant them some kind of special position that sets them above other people. It means that we recognize the natural hierarchy that God has created in human relationships, where our parents hold a position of authority over us for a good part of our lives. It's very significant that in Leviticus 19:3, where this commandment is repeated, the Israelites are told to "reverence" (NASB) their mothers and fathers—a verb that elsewhere in the Bible is used only to describe the proper attitude toward God.

The promise clause that concludes this verse is another significant link between this commandment and the first four. As Paul observes in Ephesians 6:2, this commandment is the first of the biblical laws to include a promised outcome for obedience: if you honor your parents, your days in the land will be lengthened. None of the other nine commandments holds out such a promise. It is undoubtedly significant that God makes a similar promise to the Israelite nation concerning the way they honor the Lord. If the Israelites keep his whole covenant, God promises them that they will possess the land forever (Deut. 5:33; 6:3; 11:8-9). Compare also the words of the fifth commandment to the words of Deuteronomy 30:17-18: "But if your heart turns away and you are not obedient, and if you are drawn away to bow down to other gods and worship them, I declare to you this day that you will certainly be destroyed. You will not live long in the land you are crossing the Jordan to enter and possess." The phrase "you will not live long in the land" is simply the negative version of the promise contained in the fifth commandment. We can reasonably conclude that our obligation to our parents is comparable to our obligation to God. Make no mistake about it, our attitude toward parents reflects our attitude toward authority as a whole—and by implication, it reflects our attitude toward God.

Let's briefly consider the meaning of this promise. Note that it isn't made to an individual, but rather to the entire nation of Israel. The Promised Land was God's gift to Israel as a whole, and this promise is also made to the nation as a whole. It doesn't mean that a person who honors his parents will necessarily live a long time—we all know that isn't the case. Rather, this promise means that if Israel *as a nation* honors its parents, then the nation will not be banished from the Promised Land. We can't make a direct application to individuals, but later we'll consider what this promise means for us as a society.

Like the fourth commandment, the fifth is issued in positive terms. It doesn't issue a prohibition such as, "Don't neglect your mother and father." Instead, it issues an order to honor them. Perhaps there's a subtle message here. Honoring our parents shouldn't be a burden or a constraint. It is a privilege, just like honoring God, our Creator, Sustainer, and Protector is our privilege as well.

A QUESTION OF HONOR

The principle behind the fifth commandment is the hierarchical order to creation. Our primary esteem goes to God, but after God, we are to accord honor to our parents. But what is meant by "honor"? The Hebrew verb *kabed,* "honor," gives us the noun *kabod,* which is translated "glory." Its basic meaning is "to be heavy, weighty." So honoring someone essentially means according them weight, regarding them as significant. People are often honored in the Bible. The high priest Eli honored his sons by giving them gifts (1 Sam. 2:29), and Samuel honored King Saul by accompanying him to worship (15:30). David attempted to honor the late king of the Ammonites by sending emissaries to his funeral (2 Sam. 10:2). It is also possible to honor things. God honors the place where his feet rest (Isa. 60:13) and requires that we honor the Sabbath day (58:13). We also may honor God by giving him respect (25:3), by praising his name (Ps. 22:25; Isa. 43:20), or by offering sacrifices to him (Mal. 1:6).

Your mother may not feel flattered if you tell her that you think she's "heavy," but in Old Testament times, "light" was regarded as insignificant, unworthy of notice. In fact, to make something or consider something "light" was the equivalent of cursing it: "Anyone who curses his father or mother must be put to death" (Ex. 21:17). Cursing one's parents ("making light of them") instead of honoring them ("making heavy of them") is considered a capital offense. Even today, a "lightweight" is a person who can be overlooked or treated with contempt. A "heavyweight," on the other hand, carries authority, and can only be ignored at the risk of well-being or life.

Honor is not worship. Honor is not *necessarily* obedience, even though it may well include obedience. It *is* giving persons or things a special degree of respect due to their character, their office, or their nature.

HONOR BY CHILDREN

In attempting to live out the principle behind the fifth commandment in our daily lives, a number of matters should be kept in mind. First, note that this commandment wasn't intended for children alone. Jesus acknowledged this fact in his own teachings on the fifth commandment (Mark 7:9–13), which we'll discuss below. A child's obligations to his or her parents don't end after the child grows up and moves out of the house. The ways we live out the principle of honoring our parents will change in different phases of life.

Paul wrote that one way children keep this commandment is by obeying their parents "in the Lord" (Eph. 6:1). He assures the Ephesians that this is the "right" thing to do, using a Greek word for "right" that implies something conforming to the usual custom or rule. Children, then, are to obey their parents as a matter of principle, and not based on whether their parents have earned their obedience. Children are obligated to obey, not because their parents are smarter than they are or because they'll be punished if they don't obey. Paul says that being obedient is simply the right thing to do.

In our day, this instruction sends up red flags. What if the parents are abusive? What if they are sexual predators or Fagin-types, using their children for illegal or immoral purposes? Are children still obligated to obey those kinds of parents? What if the parents aren't Christians, and they try to persuade their children away from the faith? We can imagine situations where unbelieving parents forbid their children to go to church or read the Bible, and someone tells the child that he or she must obey because the Bible says children should honor their parents. What does the child do then?

These aren't merely hypothetical questions. News accounts report many so-called "parents" who take advantage of their children or attempt to negatively influence them. I don't believe that children are obligated to do evil in obedience to their parents. Note that Paul includes the little phrase "in the Lord" in the Ephesians verse— and it's loaded with meaning. It reminds us that the principle behind the fifth commandment is one of hierarchy, or levels of authority. Highest authority belongs to God, and no human authority can countermand God's will. Just as the disciples decided to disobey when they were ordered by the Jewish high council not to preach in the name of Jesus, our first obligation is to obey God rather than any human authority (Acts 4:19; 5:39). If a child's parents try to make her or him go against the will of God, the child should disobey. Jesus was forced to disobey his own mother when she attempted to make him give up his ministry (Mark 3:21, 33–35).

Bear in mind, too, that for the Christian, none of the Ten Commandments is a binding, legal obligation. Rather, they are the standards and principles for our conduct. If we legalistically hold each other to observe the Ten Commandments, we're missing the point of the whole argument presented in the first chapter. The commandments won't save us, and they mustn't enslave us. If, in a manner unworthy of a Christian, we try to force children into submission by holding the fifth commandment over their heads, we're putting them under bondage.

More basic than obeying, children must recognize the authority of their parents. Once they recognize that authority, obedience comes naturally. Some parents strive to "break" their children into compliant little automatons. God doesn't do that to us. He allows us freedom of choice, but he expects us to respect his authority. A child who respects his or her parents' authority doesn't need to be broken or bound with rules. The best kind of love and respect is that which is freely given.

ADULTS AND HONOR

As mentioned above, the fifth commandment wasn't written just for children. Adults, too, should give honor to their parents. In fact, it's likely that this commandment was originally directed to adults rather than children. In some ancient cultures, the elderly were viewed as a burden to be pushed aside. They could be driven from the community and forced to fend for themselves or (more often) die trying. The fifth commandment forbids such treatment of our parents. Rather, we're to hold them in proper respect, recognizing the hierarchy of creation that made our parents our predecessors and acknowledging the debt we owe to them for rearing us.

One way that adult children honored their parents in ancient times was by supporting them financially. In the days before Social Security, pensions, and Medicare, the elderly often had very limited sources of income. They depended on their savings and on their children for support. Unlike our day, when children inherit the parents' property after the parents pass away, it was customary in those days for parents to distribute their wealth to their children *before* they died. (Remember the story of the Prodigal Son [Luke 15:11–32]. The lad had come to his father asking for his share of his inheritance while the father was still alive and well, albeit a little before the father would have expected.) Then, when the children had received their inheritance, they'd support the parents partly from this income. It was a system that required a good deal of trust. Once the parents had given their property to their children, they had to trust that the children would supply their needs. There's a certain poetic charm to the system. While growing up, the children had depended on their parents for everything. Now, the tables were turned—the parents would learn to depend on their children.

There's also a practical side to this arrangement. Once the kids have moved out and set up their own homes, the parents don't need all their accumulated wealth. Their needs should be much simpler. When the children are starting out in their careers and raising their own families, they could use a little financial help from their parents. So in the old days, the parents would give the children their inheritance when it would do them the most good. The retired parents then had the joy of watching the blessing that their gift would bring to their children's families.

Human nature being what it is, however, children sometimes fell down on their part of the arrangement and failed to support their parents properly. In Malachi 1:6–7, the Lord compares himself to a parent who doesn't receive proper honor from his children because the priests were bringing him second-rate sacrifices. If I'm truly like a father, God says, then you should give me the honor that I'm due. Bring me tithes and offerings that truly show me honor. The wastrel in the Prodigal Son story, too, failed to honor his father because he took his entire inheritance and squandered it on himself. His father forgave him, even though half of his retirement income had been wasted.

The most outrageous situation of disrespecting parents is described by Jesus in Mark 7:9-13. Here, Jesus talks about how the Pharisees would set aside the Law by appealing to tradition. The Law commands the Jews to honor their fathers and mothers, but the Pharisees had devised a way around that commandment. In a practice that seems to have been widely used in Jesus' day, a person could declare inherited property *corban,* meaning "devoted to God." When an item was declared *corban,* the owner vowed to receive no benefit from it—it was as if the item belonged to God. If, for example, a field was declared *corban,* the owner wouldn't harvest and sell the produce. Declaring *corban,* however, didn't mean that the owner gave the produce to the temple or the local synagogue or even to the poor. He just declared that the field was set apart, and if God wanted its produce, God could have it.

But the tradition of *corban* could be turned to self-serving ends. Not only could the owner declare something *corban* in regard to himself, he could declare it *corban* with respect to specific people. For instance, the owner, to keep his no-good son-in-law from getting his hands on certain goods, could declare those goods *corban* with respect to the son-in-law. The owner could still use them, but his son-in-law couldn't. As far as the son-in-law was concerned, the goods belonged to God. The system exploited superstition. What person would dare violate a vow made to God, even if the person hadn't taken it him- or herself? Archaeologists have unearthed an ancient Jewish tomb that bears the inscription, "Whatever one might find to his benefit in this tomb is *corban* [dedicated] to God from him who is within it." In other words, "Plunder this tomb at your own risk. Its contents belong to God!"

In the passage from Mark mentioned above, Jesus seems to be describing a particularly unsavory scheme. Adult children would inherit property from their parents, then declare that property *corban* in respect to their parents. Their parents couldn't touch it because, in their eyes, it belonged to God. The children, on the other hand, could use it freely. It was a clever way of disguising greed as piety.

So in Jesus' day, the concern about honoring one's parents was a realistic one. Unprincipled children could easily find ways to avoid their responsibilities. In our own day, the situation is rather different. We don't really expect children to give financial support to their parents. We expect parents to make provision for themselves, or we expect the government to support them. Sometimes, children will help pay the cost of a nursing home for parents—and often that's little better than no help at all.

SUPPORTING OUR PARENTS EMOTIONALLY

There are, of course, good nursing homes and bad nursing homes. When aged parents can no longer care for themselves and need a great deal of attention, placing them in a nursing home may be the best solution. It can be a decision made through loving, prayerful reflection. Too often, however, the decision to institutionalize parents is made for convenience rather than out of love. It would, the adult children argue, upset the family routine to bring the parents into the house. It would disturb the kids, put the dog out of his room. The adult child might have to quit work or cut back on hours to care for his or her parent, and the family certainly can't afford that, since they're still making payments on the new minivan! The idea of inconveniencing ourselves for the sake of our parents is inconceivable to many of us. We've apparently forgotten how much we inconvenienced *them* while we were growing up.

It is tragic that the vast majority of people in nursing homes never receive any visitors at all. My heart has been broken as I've walked through the halls of some of these institutions and had residents ask me, "Are you my son? Are you Joey?" Desperately they reach out to anyone who comes near, hoping that it might be their son or daughter, hoping that their children haven't forgotten them. Even sadder still are the individuals who have just withdrawn into themselves. They've given up hope of seeing Joey come down the hall, of seeing anyone who wants to talk to them and love them. They retreat into dreams, or memories, or catatonic states.

In our society, we don't drive our parents out into the wilderness to die by themselves, but too often, our parents do die alone. They are neglected by the very people who owe them the greatest debt. In our modern culture of convenience and in our self-indulgent society, elderly parents are often viewed as a burden to be cared for by someone else. We may be willing to make a financial investment in them by providing for their physical care, but too many people won't make the emotional investment in a loving, ongoing relationship with their parents. They honor them materially, but they don't honor them spiritually.

Certainly we recognize the difficult emotional dynamics involved in seeing one's parents become old and infirm. It embarrasses us, and we're embarrassed for them. We depended on them, idolized them, and believed they were omnipotent—and now they creep along on a cane, they ask us to repeat ourselves, they click their dentures. Maybe they can't remember how to drive a car or how to dial a telephone. It hurts to see them this way. Yet we now see them the same way that they first saw us—helpless and dependent. Life has come around full circle. We depended utterly on them for nurture, for warmth, and for love. And now, who do they have to depend on but us? Who is it more fitting that they turn to, but us?

Perhaps the greatest humiliation that any human being can experience is feeling that he or she has become an unwelcome burden. We do not honor our parents by treating them like old news.

PARENTS UNWORTHY OF HONOR

Many people ask, "What about parents who don't deserve honor?" In a commentary on Exodus, an author seemed embarrassed by the fifth commandment. He stated, in effect, that if the Ten Commandments had been written today, considering the frequent reports of child abuse, they would have included a command about parents' responsibility to their children. Obviously this scholar didn't fully appreciate the nature of the verb "to honor." The fifth commandment is about the requirements of a hierarchical relationship, not a reciprocal one. In a partnership, honor must go both ways. In a hierarchy, honor goes to those above you because of their position. Other kinds of honor can be afforded in the relationship. Parents might "honor" their children because of their achievements, or simply because of their love for them. But children must honor their parents by virtue of their position. Even if they're negligent, even if they're incompetent, even if they're abusive, they still hold the honored position in the relationship.

Don't get me wrong—I'm not saying we have to approve of undeserving parents, fawn over them, or even like them. But we mustn't refuse to honor them. If we worked under an inept manager, we would probably complain about it. We might joke about the manager behind his or her back. We would grumble that we could do the job better. Yet we would still pay that boss the honor due his or her position—that, or we would probably be looking for a new job. Such honor doesn't depend on one's performance, but only on one's position.

In college, I was involved in a Bible study group led by a young woman whose biblical knowledge wasn't as deep as my own. I often challenged her opinions, occasionally took over the discussion, and sometimes was a general nuisance. The tension between us rose as she began to cut me off any time I started to make a comment. Of course, the other members of the group weren't oblivious to the strained relations, and one of them asked to talk to me about it. I explained how difficult it was for me to listen to the leader's "shallow" explanations of some of the Bible passages. My friend expressed sympathy, but he reminded me that I simply was not the group's leader. I hadn't given the leader the respect she deserved by virtue of her position. I realized he was right. Even if I thought I knew more about the Bible, or even if I thought I could lead a discussion better than anyone else in the group, I was not the group's leader. I apologized to the leader and promised to accord her the authority she deserved.

We can't stand as judges over which parents deserve honor and which do not. Some people might consider parents bad—unworthy of honor—because they spank their children. Others would say it's those who *don't* spank who are failing their children. Some people would malign fathers who are more involved in their work than their families. Others would consider a father unworthy if he didn't work two jobs so he could put his children through college. Some people would say that any mother who doesn't breast-feed her children, or homeschool her children, or give up her career for her children is undeserving of honor. In the fifth commandment, however, God doesn't worry about such distinctions. The fifth commandment does not say, "Honor good fathers and mothers," but merely, "Honor your father and mother."

It is possible, however, that some parents so fully abrogate their responsibilities that they don't function as parents, and so do *not* merit any honor. In truth, biology alone doesn't make one a father or mother. In ancient times, and still today in some parts of the world, abandoning a child at birth is a common method of population control. In our own society, we hear stories about newborn infants found in trash dumpsters. Very likely, the people who produced these children really don't qualify as "father" and "mother." With new medical technologies, it is possible that future children will be conceived in petri dishes, raised in artificial wombs, and born from incubators. Thus, our definition of "mother" and "father" can't be based on biology alone. We aren't obliged to honor the people who provide the genetic materials for our conception if those people had nothing to do with our nurture.

Such cases are extreme, however. Most parents do raise their own children to the best of their abilities. Some parents are exploitative, some are even abusive. But, the adult children of even the worst parents should accord those parents some kind of honor, if not for their parents' sake, then for their own. As Christians, our goal is the redemption of all people—including our parents—through Jesus Christ. By according them honor—even if they don't seem to deserve it— perhaps we can help them to experience through us the love and forgiveness of Christ. Perhaps they can learn and grow into more godly people.

Yet, even if they don't, it is essential for our sakes that we forgive our parents and attempt to do them honor. Adults who carry a grudge about the way they were raised, who refuse to talk to their parents, are often sad and bitter. Just as we can't really be whole unless we have a relationship with our Creator, it is difficult for us to be at peace with ourselves unless we have peace with our parents. We should learn to forgive them, move beyond our hurt, and build a new relationship with them.

FOLLOW THE PRINCIPLE—AND LIVE

The principle of the fifth commandment, then, is to accord honor to our parents as we accord honor to God. We are to recognize the hierarchy that God has ordained in creation, a hierarchy that gives God authority over all things and gives parents authority over their children. Such honor involves respect and obedience when we're young, and respect, emotional support, and perhaps even economic provision when our parents grow older.

God gives a promise to the nation that obeys this commandment: they will have many days in the land that God gives them. The nation that neglects its parents will lose its right to God's gift of land. We no longer, of course, live under the kind of government that the ancient Israelites did. Our nation isn't the object of God's special attention and favor. Yet one must wonder if the principle associated with the promise and the gift might not apply to us. If we, as a society and a culture, neglect our elderly parents—treating them with contempt, looking upon them with embarrassment, responding with callousness and greed instead of love and compassion—do we put our nation at risk of God's judgment?

The words of the prophet Malachi seem especially appropriate: "See, I will send you the prophet Elijah before that great and dreadful day of the LORD comes. He will turn the hearts of the fathers to their children, and the hearts of the children to their fathers; or else I will come and strike the land with a curse" (4:5-6). In one sense, the curse is already with us in the epidemic of neglected and forgotten parents. And, of course, we reap what we sow. Those who forget their parents today may well be the lonely ones tomorrow. What might God do to turn us from our hedonistic lifestyles? Perhaps God will strike us with some kind of plague—or perhaps the seeds for our judgment may be found in our own self-centered attitudes.

QUESTIONS FOR REFLECTION

1. How would you define "mother" and "father"? What do you think are the most important characteristics of the parental role?
2. In what ways is your relationship with your parents like your relationship with God? In what ways is it different?
3. Do you consider your relationship with your parents a good one? Does the quality of your relationship affect the honor you accord them?
4. Do you think the biblical model of children supporting their parents is a good one? How might we implement such a system today?
5. As life spans increase, the number of older Americans grows. How much responsibility do you think the government should assume in the care of the elderly? How much responsibility falls on the elderly themselves? How much falls on their children?
6. Do you agree that even bad parents deserve honor? What standard would you use to decide who should receive honor and who shouldn't?

e i g h t

Murder and Respect

You shall not murder.
—Exodus 20:13

THE ISLAND OF DR. MOREAU may not be the most famous tale from H. G. Wells, but it may well be his most disturbing work. Born in England in 1866, Wells quaffed deeply from the spirit of optimism that was characteristic of the era before the turn of the century. In his youth, Wells was a socialist and evolutionist, believing that the human species would, with time and education, overcome all its moral and social ills. After working for a while as a teacher, he decided to try his hand at writing. His book *The Time Machine* made him almost an overnight success, and *War of the Worlds* and *The Invisible Man* cemented his reputation as a master of science fiction.

The captivating novel *The Island of Dr. Moreau* was produced fairly early in Wells's career, while he still held to his youthful idealism. And yet its tone is unrelentingly dark. It is the story of Pendrick, a castaway who is brought to a tiny island inhabited by a brilliant scientist, Dr. Moreau, and his physician assistant. Dr. Moreau has secluded himself so that he may continue his animal experimentation, free from the prying eyes of squeamish society. Using excruciatingly painful surgery, drugs, and blood transfusions, Moreau has succeeded in transforming animals into different forms and even altering their mental processes. His ultimate goal is to transform lower animals into creatures indistinguishable from human beings—a goal he hasn't quite reached, for the "Beast People" he created still display a bit of the beast. The leopard man still acts a great deal like the killer cat. The ape man seems almost human, but chatters nonsensically about things he only pretends to understand, things he calls "Big Thinks." The sloth man, ox man, and some of the others are slow and dull-witted.

The Beast People live together in a compound on the island. There, they learn how to live by the law that Dr. Moreau has given to them: "Not to go on all fours; *that* is the Law. Are we not Men? Not to suck up drink; *that* is the Law. Are we not Men? Not to eat flesh or fish; *that* is the Law. Are we not Men?" The Beast People hold Dr. Moreau and his law in superstitious awe. Through the law, their beastly natures are kept under a tenuous control. Any who disobey the law are taken back to Moreau's laboratory for further agonizing experimentation—a prospect that terrifies the creatures more than death.

Trouble erupts on the island when the leopard man transgresses the law and begins killing rabbits. When his crime is discovered, the other Beast People react with a furious bloodlust, hunting down and attacking the transgressor. Later, a puma woman escapes from the lab and actually kills the doctor himself. Pendrick tries to maintain order, but with the threat of the doctor's experimentation removed, the law loses its bite. The fragile veneer of civilization that Moreau had created breaks down among the Beast People, and those with carnivorous backgrounds revert into fierce killers.

The most disturbing thing about Wells's story is that, as he hints from time to time in the novel, he is not writing about fictional Beast People so much as about actual human society. Wells seems to say that (in spite of his own professed views on humanity's perfectibility) beneath the surface, we're all little better than beasts. It's the law, and law alone, that keeps us from killing one another. Set our basic natures free, and we're capable of the most bestial forms of behavior. Indeed, when Wells's hero is rescued from the island, he finds it hard to bear human company. All around him, he sees reminders of the Beast People. The cold stares of the rougher types remind him of the leopard man; a minister's sermon reminds him of the ape man's "Big Thinks"; the dull eyes of train passengers bring to mind the vacant stares of the more phlegmatic Beast People. *The Island of Dr. Moreau* clearly implies that human beings are merely animals, only pretending to be something better.

HUMAN BEINGS AS KILLERS

If Wells is right, human beings are killers by nature. We act like animals because we *are* animals, driven by instincts while barely restrained by laws. The Bible teaches that such an assessment of human nature is only partly true. Yes, human beings are creatures of the earth, like all of God's other animal creations. We have some instinctual behaviors—the desire to breathe, to eat, to reproduce. But human beings are unique from other creatures because we are created in God's image. We are set apart from other animals, and set above them, as well. Yes, we're a fallen species, separated from God and hampered from reaching our potential by our inborn sinfulness. Yet, we still bear the stamp of the divine, evident in our sense of beauty, our remarkable creativity, and our impulse to worship.

I don't believe that human beings are natural-born killers. There are, to be sure, pathological murderers who take life for the pleasure of the act. But the people I know who have taken a life, in war or by accident, have generally been haunted by the experience. Most of us take no pleasure in killing. Even most hunters, I find, don't really enjoy killing. They enjoy the hunt and the test of their skills against the elements and the animals. But most hunters rationalize the killing as a humane act—the animals would have suffered a much worse death by starvation or disease if they hadn't fallen quickly to a merciful bullet.

Though we don't enjoy killing, it is ironic that our species is quite good at it. According to one source, pound for pound, the puma is the most efficient killer in the animal kingdom. She has keen eyes that allow her to spot prey from a distance. She's capable of great bursts of speed over short distances, so she can overtake her prey on the run. Unlike the lion, which claws its prey until it collapses or overpowers it with brute strength, the puma trips its victim. Then, with a single bite to the neck, she kills. The puma is a model of efficiency. But what puma could extinguish thousands of lives with a single blow? What big cat could drop death on a hundred thousand men, women, and children with a single press of a button or flick of a switch? When it comes to efficient killing, the human race excels.

Humans are not "natural" killers. We don't have the speed of a leopard, the claws of a lion, or the teeth of a wolf. But original sin makes us self-centered and irresponsible. On the other hand, the very faculties given us by our Creator that make us lords of creation also make us very good at killing. We are intelligent, creative, and adaptable. The one faculty that makes us especially adept at murder is the ability to deceive ourselves. A common rationalization is "dehumanizing" the victims—seeing them as something less than people. Vietnam and Operation Desert Storm veterans tell me that they never thought of the people they shot at as human beings. They saw them only as targets.

Violent aggressors throughout history have used similar rationalizations to justify their actions. The European-descended pioneers in early America demonized the Native Americans in the days of Western expansion. By calling them savages or portraying them as animals, killing them would seem less like murder. The Nazis, too, dehumanized the Jews, and thus justified the slaughter of 6 million. Similar arguments are used today by some advocates of abortion on demand: "It's only a fetus," they say. "It's not really a person, so we can do with it as we please."

THE PROHIBITION AGAINST KILLING

Because of—or in spite of—our cultivated talent for killing, God addressed it in the Ten Commandments. With the sixth commandment, we pass completely from our "religious" obligations to God, to our obligations to human society. The most fundamental consideration in human society is the right to life. We can't get along with each other if we don't recognize each other's right to exist. If we can't get past that point, every other question is moot.

This change in subject matter is once again accompanied by a change in form. The next three commandments are very brief, consisting in the original Hebrew text of only two words. The ninth commandment says only a little more. The last commandment is still fairly terse, but it includes a list of examples. What might have prompted this change of form? Perhaps for the people of Moses' day, these commandments seemed more self-explanatory than the others. They do, after all, tend to reflect general cultural norms. The vast majority of people around the world would agree that it's not right to kill your neighbor, or steal from him, or sleep with his wife. So, perhaps God felt that these commandments didn't need elaboration at the time they were originally given.

The spare wording of the sixth, seventh, and eighth commandments, however, makes them subject in our day to wide interpretation. The words "You shall not kill" have been used to argue for pacifism, for banning the death penalty, for prohibition of animal research, even for vegetarianism. Indeed, the English wording could be interpreted in all these ways. In fact, it could be argued that the sixth commandment prohibits eating carrots and onions, since a plant must be killed in order to harvest these particular vegetables. One might even argue against taking penicillin or washing one's hands—killing even a germ is still killing.

The Hebrew wording, however, is more specific than the English translations. Like the English word "murder," the Hebrew verb used in the sixth commandment specifically designates the killing of human beings. It is used only in cases of violent death—not necessarily intentional, but always violent. It is never used to describe the execution of criminals or the killing of enemies in war. Thus the Jews understood the original wording of this commandment quite narrowly. No one argued that the Law prohibited capital punishment. The fact is, the Bible prescribed capital punishment for many offenses. The ancient Israelites felt no compunctions about waging war, even wars in which they were the aggressors. The sixth commandment, as they understood it, referred only to cases of murder and manslaughter.

MURDER AND HUMAN DIGNITY

The sixth commandment includes no rationale for prohibiting murder, but other Bible passages clearly explain why murder is wrong. It has nothing to do with preserving social order, or upholding peace, or even doing to others as you would have them do to you. The Bible's rationale is much more fundamental, and it was given before the Ten Commandments were ever expressed in words. It is found near the beginning of the book of Genesis, in the story of the Great Flood. According to Genesis 6:13, the reason God decided to destroy humanity was because human beings had filled the earth with violence. So when Noah, his family, and the animals came forth from the ark, God gave them explicit instructions on how to avoid future calamity (Gen. 9:1–17). God repeated the commands that he had given to Adam and Eve—human beings were to reign over creation, subdue it, and fill the earth. Some new instructions were given as well. Before the Flood, God allowed people to eat vegetables only. Now, human beings were permitted to kill and eat any creature of the earth. Only one creature was to remain inviolable. In Genesis 9:6, God says, "Whoever sheds the blood of man, by man shall his blood be shed; for in the image of God has God made man."

God didn't direct this command only to Noah and his family, but to all the creatures that came out of the ark. The death penalty applied to any person or animal guilty of killing a human being. The reason for this special prohibition is simply because human beings are special. We are different from any other created thing because we bear the image of God. No person has the right to take a human life, because the murderer would be striking against the very image of God on the Earth.

The basic reason for the prohibition for killing, then, is one of respect—first and foremost respect for God, because God's nature is still reflected in each human being. Killing another person is an insult to God, just like spitting at the president's portrait would be an insult to the president. Second, murder is prohibited out of respect for human dignity. We are the most glorious masterpiece of God's creative genius. We are not merely animals, trying to act like something better.

We *are* something better. The image of God that dwells in each of us makes us more valuable than the sparrow, more clever than the monkey, more majestic than the lion. We are unique and infinitely more valuable than any other created thing.

That God created humans as the supreme beings on earth carries enormous implications. Nothing in creation is more valuable than the human species. No other created thing, no human government, no philosophy, can be considered more important than a human being. The very idea is starkly at odds with the spirit of our age. We live in an age when humanity is increasingly devalued. The very abundance of human life has cheapened its worth. Today we speak less about the sanctity of human life than about the "quality" of life. Society considers some kinds of human life to possess intrinsically more quality than other kinds. A Down's Syndrome child, some would argue, has a lower quality of life than an artistic genius. A paraplegic has less quality of life than a person with two good legs. For those whose lives are deemed to have less quality, our society increasingly considers death an acceptable alternative.

To date, the very young and the very old have suffered the most from this trend. Unborn human life can now be discarded for the sake of convenience. What quality of life, some argue, would an unwanted child have? The chronically or terminally ill can be euthanized. A comfortable death is considered more important than the continuation of life. The euthanasia laws of some European countries are worded so vaguely that doctors have been allowed to kill terminally ill patients in order to free hospital beds for other patients. The prevalent cheapening of life threatens anyone whom society decides lacks quality of life. How long will it be before our social norms calculate that the homeless are better off dead and are incapable of deciding for themselves if their lives have sufficient quality to merit continuation?

Some think we should take steps to limit human population growth. We must be responsible citizens and stewards of this planet. Yet we must not allow ourselves to lose our sense of wonder at the majesty of the human race. God takes great delight in every one of us and considers us extremely valuable, no matter how little "quality"—as human beings define the word—an individual life might possess.

JESUS ON MURDER

Jesus makes his stand on the dignity of human life clear in his own discussion of the sixth commandment. He states:

> You have heard that it was said to the people long ago, "Do not murder, and anyone who murders will be subject to judgment." But I tell you that anyone who is angry with his brother will be subject to judgment. Again, anyone who says to his brother, "Raca," is answerable to the Sanhedrin. But anyone who says, "You fool!" will be in danger of the fire of hell. (Matt. 5:21–22)

Contrary to some current opinions, Jesus isn't opposed to the Ten Commandments. He's not about to negate the words of the sixth commandment and say it no longer applies to his followers. Rather, Jesus looks with sharp perception beyond the mere words of the commandment and expounds on its *intention*. It is likely that most people in Jesus' day felt safe concerning the sixth commandment because they had never killed anyone. The sixth commandment, they could smugly conclude, had nothing to do with them. But Jesus confronts his audience with the principle behind the commandment. If the sixth commandment is really about respect for the image of God, then not killing our neighbor is the absolute *minimum* requirement of the Law. The spirit of the Law takes us much farther and addresses our attitudes toward others.

Jesus gives three examples to emphasize the real significance of the sixth commandment. The first example deals with our emotional response to others. The other two examples deal with how we express those emotions. These two epithets are not meant to exhaust the ways in which one can disrespect God's image in one's neighbors. Rather, these specific examples are designed to illustrate our attitudes in real-life situations. Through these examples, we can consider the implications of the commandment in concrete rather than theoretical terms.

JESUS ON ANGER

Jesus begins with the problem of anger. Of the items mentioned in the above passage from Matthew, anger most often affects us, because none of us is immune to anger. When ill-conceived anger is directed at another, when we harbor it in our souls, it can be the spiritual equivalent of murder. It's disrespectful of God's image in our neighbors. So, Jesus warns that anger puts us in danger of standing before a judge. He is speaking figuratively, of course, for no court would try a man or woman simply because he or she was angry with someone. Jesus' words are designed to underscore the similarities between anger and the crime of murder.

Nowhere does God command us not to get angry. Paul wrote, "In your anger do not sin" (Eph. 4:26), so obviously there's such a thing as non-sinful anger. We often read about God's anger with sinful humanity in the Old Testament (Exod. 32:10-12; Num. 11:1; Deut. 32:19; Josh. 7:1; Jer. 10:10; etc.). Jesus himself became angry on several occasions as recorded in the Gospels. He had good reason to get angry with the Pharisees, who used people for their own selfish ends (Mark 3:1-6), and who often made it difficult for the common people to receive the good news of salvation (Matthew 23). He was also very angry with the moneychangers in the temple (John 2:12-16), and he gave vent to his anger in an act of violence.

So anger isn't necessarily wrong. God created anger as an intrinsic part of our biological makeup. It is a chemical reaction, a firing of certain neurons in the brain. Indeed, anger is one of the most basic emotions. Zoologists observe that fish seem incapable of love or sorrow, but they do seem capable of anger. Anger can stir us to fight when fight is necessary. Consider a mother rabbit defending her young. Her anger makes her capable of driving off larger, hungry predators. Anger empowers her and motivates her and gets her adrenaline flowing. That adrenaline rush quickens her reaction time, strengthens her muscles, and dulls her sensitivity to pain. Anger can work the same way with us. It can be essential for the survival of the species.

So, there's definitely such a thing as good anger. In Jesus, we see an example of the proper use of anger. Good anger burns for someone else's sake. We feel "righteous indignation" when another individual is insulted or wounded or barred from experiencing God's goodness. Good anger fueled the abolition of slavery, the civil rights movement, and the anti-abortion movement. Anger, too, flares when God's glory is besmirched. We have both a right and a responsibility to defend God's honor when souls may be lost due to someone's blasphemy or heresy. Good anger might, however, impel us to do bad things, like oppressing or killing those who believe differently than we do. It is not, however, the anger that is bad; it's our wisdom and charity that should be called into question.

Some anger is neither good nor bad—it simply *is*. If someone spits in our faces, calls us names, or cuts us off at the highway on-ramp, we might well get angry. Such anger isn't necessarily sinful. Remember, God created anger. It's the way that we handle anger—or the way that it handles us—that causes us to sin. Currently, there's a great deal of talk about "road rage." Drivers become angry because someone has been thoughtless or discourteous to them on the highway. Instead of venting their anger with words, some drivers try to take action against the person who has wronged them. These angry drivers pursue the offenders at high speeds, try to cut them off in traffic, maybe even force them off the road. Road rage has been blamed for many traffic fatalities. Obviously, that's not the best way to deal with anger. Anger is a natural, God-given emotion; but like most of God's gifts, if we overindulge it, our anger can have disastrous consequences. We need to master our anger rather than allow it to master us.

Finally, there is anger that is always bad. Bad anger is directed not at what someone has done, but at who someone *is*. We are angry because someone is too smart, or too beautiful, or too successful. We are angry because someone is the wrong color or lives in the wrong neighborhood. We attack because someone is considered "slow" or "clumsy" or "stupid." Such anger can arise when we generalize a person's flaws and inflate those flaws until they blot out all the person's good qualities. This kind of generalization often occurs when marriages begin to break down. A little incident, like socks left in the middle of the bedroom floor, creates a stream of feelings that flow from the specific offense—"He doesn't put his socks in the hamper"—to the broader indictment—"He's a lazy slob!"

Another type of generalization arises from our own insecurities. Looking down on another person helps us feel better about ourselves. For instance, I counseled a man who seemed to have a pathological hatred of homosexuals—the mere mention of homosexuality could send him into an angry tirade. Our conversations eventually revealed that he himself was dealing with homosexual feelings, and these feelings were both frightening and repulsive to him. His anger was as much with himself, as with practicing homosexuals.

No doubt anger of this type, directed at another person's identity, "bleeds over" into hatred. As John writes in 1 John 3:15, those who hate other people are on a par with murderers. Hating a person demonstrates, as surely as does murder, a lack of respect for God's image in that person.

JESUS ON INSULTS

In an earlier chapter, we discussed how insulting words might affect a person's self-image. Jesus obviously is aware of the danger of words. Words that vent anger toward another undercut the image of God in that person, which constitutes "character assault"—the verbal equivalent of murder.

In the Matthew passage above, Jesus mentions a then common insult—"Raca" (or more accurately, *raqa*). This Aramaic word comes from the verb *raq*, meaning "to be vain, worthless." It is the equivalent of saying, "You good-for-nothing!" It wasn't a particularly harsh epithet, but it was cutting. Again, it attacks a person for who he or she is rather than something in particular that person might have done. Such language, Jesus warned, was bad enough to bring you before the Sanhedrin, the Jewish senate. Generally, the Sanhedrin would try only the most serious cases, those that carried the death penalty. So calling someone worthless, in Jesus' eyes, is a very serious crime.

A person who called another a fool, however, had committed an even greater sin. He wasn't just liable to human jurisdiction. Such a sin, Jesus said, put him in danger of hell fire—a far worse judgment than anything the Sanhedrin could pass down.

One should exercise care, however, not to take this passage too literally. Jesus mentions these punishments for the purpose of illustration only, not because someone would literally be sent to hell for calling a neighbor a fool. We know this to be the case because of the previous comment, that someone who calls his neighbor "worthless" would be subject to judgment by the Sanhedrin. The fact is, the Sanhedrin would never have tried someone for calling a person worthless—it only judged the most serious criminal acts. Furthermore, we know from the gospel that the words we use do not damn us. The only sin that sends us to hell is the sin of unbelief, of refusing the grace offered through Jesus Christ our Lord. By bringing up the threat of hell, Jesus hoped to impress on us the seriousness of using such insults. When we call someone a fool, we denigrate the value of a person created in the image of God, a person whom God loves dearly. We are saying that someone for whom Christ died has no value, which is an opinion that God doesn't share.

C. S. Lewis encouraged us to consider every person a potential spiritual giant. The seeds of spiritual greatness reside within each individual because, no matter how distorted it might have become, the image of God resides there. How embarrassing it would be to call your neighbor a worthless good-for-nothing today, then when you get to heaven, find that he had been given the seat of honor beside Jesus Christ.

FIGHTING THE GOOD FIGHT

The wisdom of Jesus' teaching becomes evident when we consider the advice of marriage counselors in regard to "fighting fair." There's a difference, they maintain, between a good fight and a bad fight. In a good fight, a couple argues about an issue and how it makes each of them feel. For instance, in a good fight, the wife might say, "You didn't take your plate off the table again tonight. When you don't put away your plate, it makes me feel like you're taking advantage of me." Compare these words to the first punch in a bad fight: "You didn't take your plate off the table again. You're nothing but a lazy bum!"

The difference is obvious. In the first example, the wife kept to the issue—that she was hurt by what her husband had done. She didn't even argue that what her husband did was necessarily wrong in and of itself. She simply reported how it had made her feel. In the second example, she generalized her husband's specific behavior into a statement about his character. She attacked his worth by placing a label on him, defining his whole person as "a lazy bum." When a couple argues in the latter fashion, their marriage is in serious peril. Respect between the partners is gone. If the marriage is to be saved, respect must be restored, and anger must be redirected from the spouse to the spouse's actions.

Likewise, God wants us to regard others with the respect due them as children of God, made in God's image. If we are angry with other people, we should be angry because of their specific behaviors, not because of who they are. If we want to express our dissatisfaction with them, we don't attack their identities. For instance, when someone cuts you off in traffic, you might want to say, "He's an idiot." It would be more accurate, and more godly, to say, "What he did was thoughtless." You might be tempted to call your shrewish wife a witch, but unless she rides a broom and worships Satan, it's more pleasing to God (and your marriage would have a better chance of surviving) if you tell her that you feel hurt when she nags and belittles you.

HUMAN DIGNITY

At this point, the subject appears to have gone far afield of the sixth commandment. It seems a stretch to associate killing your neighbor with calling your wife a witch. I cannot emphasize too strongly, however, that the same principle applies to both situations. We need to treat every human being with respect, because all humans bear the image of God. God doesn't prohibit murder simply because he wants us to be "nice." He doesn't prohibit murder merely because he fears the breakdown of social order. He prohibits murder because he places more value on us than we place on ourselves. Let us handle one another with care, recognizing the dignity that dwells in each and every human life.

QUESTIONS FOR REFLECTION

1. In what ways are human beings similar to animals? In what ways are we different? How do you see God's image manifest within our species?
2. When there are conflicts between human existence and the existence of other species, should the human race always come first?
3. How does consideration for God's image influence our decisions regarding the morality of abortion? Of euthanasia? Of the death penalty?
4. How do you distinguish between anger at what someone has done and anger at who someone *is*?
5. Do you see any similarities between murder and name calling? Have you ever felt "verbally assassinated"?

nine

The Faithful Heart

You shall not commit adultery.
—Exodus 20:14

IF THE SEVENTH COMMANDMENT could talk, it might say, "I don't get no respect." Like comedian Rodney Dangerfield, the commandment prohibiting adultery doesn't seem to be taken very seriously. Adultery is regarded as almost a normal, acceptable, and even humorous part of human existence. And this attitude isn't especially modern. "Cheating," as it's euphemistically called, was a major theme of Chaucer's comical *Canterbury Tales*—written in the fourteenth century. Playwrights from the Middle Ages and the Renaissance period induced many a chuckle with the philandering husband or the wandering wife. And, of course, adultery has been part of the standard repertoire for most twentieth-century comedians.

Television has made such bawdy humor the true property of the masses. The hit series *M*A*S*H*, in its early years, had many laughs at the expense of marital faithfulness. The show's writers seemed to feel that the first casualty of war is fidelity. The *M*A*S*H* doctors and nurses, an exceptionally randy bunch, regarded extramarital sex as a given—and if anyone expressed otherwise, he or she was labeled hypocritical. To its credit, the creators of the show seemed to develop a pang of conscience eventually, and the show expressed a more responsible attitude toward unfaithfulness in its later seasons. Then the FOX network introduced *Married: With Children,* a show that obsessed about illicit sex to a degree never before seen on the small screen. The show's main character, Al Bundy, read porno magazines, hung out at "the nudie bar," fantasized about every attractive woman he encountered, and yet vigorously spurned his wife's efforts to initiate sex. The show set new low standards for TV morality, but it was soon outdone. Other networks rushed to become competitive in the "sleaze ratings."

On the big screen, adultery has been given more serious treatment. Hollywood blockbusters like "The Piano" or "The Bridges of Madison County" portray adultery as a legitimate escape from an unhappy marriage. The plot lines manipulate viewers into cheering for the adulterers, applauding their breech of vows and trust. The message of the scripts are clear: everyone deserves a little happiness; everyone has the right to enjoy intimacy with a person who truly loves him or her. Even the Bible says, "Love covers a multitude of sins"!

The assault against marital fidelity would be bad enough if everyone were merely watching other people have extramarital affairs. But, a lot of people have bought into the fantasy that forbidden fruit is sweetest. Poll results vary widely on the percentage of spouses who actually "cheat," but some reputable pollsters report that two out of five married men and one out of five married women have cheated on their spouses at some time in their marriages. Even allowing that the analysts might have inflated the numbers somewhat, it is clear that many people do not remain faithful throughout their married lives. On the brighter side, though, all the polls agree that most people never have more than one extramarital encounter. Once adulterers discover that the reality doesn't live up to the fantasy, or they're too nervous to perform, or too guilt-ridden to look at themselves in the mirror, most settle back down with their spouses and vow never to be so foolish again. They've made a harsh discovery: adultery isn't glamorous or liberating. It is shameful, imprisoning, and sinful.

THE ISRAELITE UNDERSTANDING OF ADULTERY

Like the sixth commandment, the seventh commandment doesn't waste words. Only two words are necessary in the original Hebrew to express the idea, "Don't cheat on your spouse." Once again, modern people might consider this commandment a little ambiguous. Just what constitutes adultery? Does it mean any sexual relations outside the boundaries of marriage? Or does this commandment apply to married people only?

The Israelites understood the meaning of this commandment very narrowly. To them, it meant only that a married person was not to have sexual relations with another married person who was not his or her spouse. If a married man had sexual relations with an unmarried, unbetrothed woman, the Israelites didn't consider it adultery. There were no laws in the Old Testament prohibiting a married man from visiting a prostitute, even though the Bible clearly frowns on the practice (see Lev. 19:29; 21:9). If the female participant wasn't a prostitute, the law required that the man pay her father her dowry and take the woman as his wife (Exod. 22:16; Deut. 22:28–29). If the woman was betrothed, the situation was considered the same as if she were already married. If the woman was raped, the man was stoned to death; if she was seduced, then both partners were executed (Deut. 22:23–27).

Why such a narrow understanding of adultery? To the ancient Israelites, the main concern was protection of family property. An Israelite man wouldn't want his wife sleeping with another man primarily because he wanted the assurance that all children in his household were his offspring. These children would one day inherit his property, and he wanted to be certain that the property remained within his own family line. The Israelite husband's concern brings to mind the habit of the cuckoo bird. The cuckoo's mother lays its eggs in the nest of another species. The cuckoos hatch first and push the other eggs out of the nest. The baby cuckoos then receive all the food and attention of the mother bird. The Israelite men didn't want any cuckoos in their nests—illegitimate children who would dispossess their own biological offspring.

This understanding of adultery doesn't sound particularly spiritual. But think of it from the ancient Israelite's point of view. His understanding of the afterlife wasn't as profound as the one that we've been privileged to receive. The Old Testament downplays the idea of life after death. Jesus hadn't risen from the dead yet, so the ancient Israelites had little evidence that death is a defeated foe. In Old Testament times, then, a lot of emphasis was placed on having children who could remember you and carry on your name and the family traditions. Dying childless was considered the greatest of catastrophes—a sure sign of God's displeasure (Lev. 20:20-21; Deut. 7:14). An illegitimate child in the house was considered a shame to the husband and a potential threat to his posterity.

What Did God Intend?

But, just because the ancient Israelites understood the prohibition of adultery as a protection of their posterity, that doesn't mean that God had the same understanding. There is sometimes a big difference between the way God allows us to live at one time, and the way God actually *wants* us to live. Jesus made this fact clear in his teaching on divorce (Matt. 19:1-12). According to Deuteronomy 24:1, a man was permitted to divorce his wife if he found "something indecent about her." In Jesus' time, there was a debate between two famous rabbis on what constituted "something indecent." Hillel said a man could only divorce his wife if she was unfaithful to him. Shammai said that he could divorce her for anything that displeases him—even if she burned his dinner! The Pharisees came to Jesus and asked his opinion. Jesus answered that God never had wanted people to divorce at all. Rather, when a couple married, they became one flesh. What God had joined was meant to be eternal. The Pharisees then asked why Moses allowed a man to divorce his wife. Jesus told them, "Moses permitted you to divorce your wives because your hearts were hard. But it was not this way from the beginning" (Matt. 19:8). In other words, God allows divorce only because our sinfulness requires it. It is not his best plan for our lives.

Clearly, we have to make a distinction between what God ultimately wants for us, and what God is willing for a time to put up with. For a while, God was willing to put up with the Israelites' understanding of adultery. God didn't want men visiting prostitutes. There are some clues in the Bible about God's real thoughts on the matter. For instance, in Leviticus 19:29, the Israelites are commanded not to let their daughters become prostitutes, lest the land be filled with wickedness. So the Bible does associate prostitution with wickedness. In Leviticus 21:9, God commands that if a priest's daughter becomes a prostitute, she is to be executed because of the shame she brings on her father. The Proverbs, too, warn young men not to visit prostitutes (6:24–26; 23:26–28). God's view on polygamy is presented with a little more subtlety, but I think the disapproval is just as apparent. The first polygamist, a descendant of murderous Cain, is also a murderer (Gen. 4:19–24). Other stories of polygamy always feature strife or trouble (e.g., Sarah and Hagar, Gen. 16:1–6; 21:8–10; Leah and Rachel, Gen. 29:31–30:24; Solomon's wives, 1 Kings 11:1–13). God was willing to allow these customs to continue for a season, while gently leading his people into a greater understanding of his perfect will.

Many people in Jesus' day tried to figure out what the Law allowed them to get away with, but Jesus came promoting a different attitude. The issue, he argues, is not what the Law says—the issue is what the Law really intends. This important distinction is still made today in constitutional law. Some legal theorists argue that the intention of the Constitution's authors is more important than the actual wording. So when the Constitution says, "Congress shall make no law promoting the establishment of a religion, or prohibiting the free exercise thereof," these theorists would argue that the statement must be understood in light of its framers' intent. The intent, they would say, was not to prohibit *states* or *communities* from promoting a certain religion, but only the federal government. The Constitution, they argue, says nothing about a nativity scene in front of city hall.

Others would argue that the words themselves are more important than their original meaning. The Constitution is then a dynamic document that changes with the times. The words are interpreted with no consideration of their authors' original intent. These theorists would argue that even though the authors of the Constitution had never intended to ban prayer in public schools, the words of the Constitution can be interpreted in just such a way.

On the seventh commandment, Jesus clearly takes the "intention" position. And who better than Jesus to expound on what was in God's mind when God gave the Ten Commandments? The intention of the Law actually presents us with a more challenging standard than does concentrating on its words. Words can be manipulated into lists of what we can get away with. But God's original plan presents us with a higher standard, a higher mark for which we may strive—the mark of perfection.

JESUS ON ADULTERY

For Jesus, the principle behind the commandment, "You shall not commit adultery" wasn't property rights, it was relationships. Jesus clarified his position by appealing to God's purpose in creating the institution of marriage. Genesis 2 tells us that God created a single human being, unique and above all the creatures of earth. Soon, God decided that it wasn't good for the human being to be alone. Of all the animals in creation, there was none that could be a suitable partner for the human. So God took a rib from the human's side and crafted another human being. Where there had been one human, now there were two, male and female.

God created marriage so that human beings would have an ally in life who "corresponds" to us (Gen. 2:18). With such an ally, we can enjoy intimacy unlike any that we might have with the other creatures on earth. We can be naked and unashamed, as Adam and Eve were in the Garden (v. 25). In other words, we can let our innermost secrets show, being open with each other in a way that we're open with no one else. Marriage can help us fulfill one of our deepest human longings—the desire to be known and accepted for who we are. In a marriage that's functioning the way God had intended, we should be able to find that unconditional positive regard that most people only experience from their dogs.

The sex act is designed to be part of the process of learning about and accepting one another. In the Hebrew Bible, the most common expression for sexual intercourse is to "know" someone: "Adam knew

Eve his wife and she conceived" (Gen. 4:1 KJV). In the sex act, we open ourselves up fully to another person. We place ourselves in our most vulnerable position. Our emotions are completely released; our restraint is abandoned. Sex grows from intimacy, and it reinforces intimacy as well. It's a normal part of a properly functioning marriage.

Thus, the main purpose of marriage is intimacy. Anything that threatens to undermine the openness and trust that should character-ize our marriages is sin, and a violation of God's original purpose. Faithfulness to our spouses must begin in our hearts, not in our bod-ies. Our hearts and minds are the true wellspring of intimacy; our bodies only follow their leads.

For some people, Jesus' teaching on adultery seems the harshest passage in the entire Bible. His words cut to the very heart of the matter:

> You have heard that it was said, "Do not commit adultery." But I tell you that anyone who looks at a woman lustfully has already committed adultery with her in his heart. If your right eye causes you to sin, gouge it out and throw it away. It is better for you to lose one part of your body than for your whole body to be thrown into hell. And if your right hand causes you to sin, cut it off and throw it away. It is better for you to lose one part of your body than for your whole body to go into hell. (Matt. 5:27–30)

Tough words! How many people have tortured themselves, sure they were guilty of adultery in their hearts? When I was in seminary, my New Testament professor told the story of a man he had known in China many years ago. At that time, the professor was an interpreter for an American missionary who spoke little Chinese. A native Christian had come to the missionary deeply distraught. Through the interpreter, he explained that he had read Jesus' words on adultery and felt very guilty. He said he had prayed until the tears flowed, but it seemed that he couldn't help noticing attractive women. How, he asked, could he be delivered from this sin? The missionary answered, "Tell him he must pray harder!" The future professor was shocked. "I can't tell him that!"

he said. "This man is already tormented to the point of going crazy!"

The professor then explained that he studied the meaning of the Greek word translated "lust" and concluded that the word didn't mean "to find someone attractive." Rather, it means "a will to possess" a thing. In other words, lust isn't so much about a hormonal surge as about an act of our wills, an intention to have something or someone for ourselves. It's not a passing whim of fancy or a harmless appreciation for someone's good looks. Lust is persistent. Jesus didn't say, "You should never find anyone attractive but your spouse." Rather, he seems to say, "Once the act of unfaithfulness is entertained in the mind, it's as good as done in the body." Adultery doesn't happen by accident. It starts as an act of our wills. According to Jesus, once we decide to entertain lustful thoughts—whether we are led to the physical act of adultery or the whole affair remains in the realm of fantasy—we're already committing adultery in our hearts.

The reason behind Jesus' position is simple: desire for someone other than your spouse threatens the bond of trust and intimacy that is the basis of a good marriage. God created marriage so that we can be open with one another, naked and unashamed. When a marriage partner engages in persistent fantasy about others, it undermines the dreamer's acceptance of his or her own spouse. Instead of appreciating a spouse for him- or herself, fantasizers can find themselves wishing they were married to someone else—or at least sleeping with someone else. It is ironic that, on this point at least, the show *Married: With Children* is dead on. Al Bundy, with his porno magazines, his nudie bar, and his sexual fantasies, has little interest in a physical relationship with his wife. Their marriage is barely a marriage at all. As distorted as this caricature might be, it may well be similar to many marriages in modern society.

SETTING LIMITS OR ESTABLISHING PRINCIPLES?

By fixing adultery in the heart, Jesus cuts through the question of where to set limits. We don't have to wonder where expressions of affection for persons to whom we are not married cross the line and become sinful—it's the state of our heart, not the position of our hands, that settles the question. Most often, it's unmarried people who have these kinds of concerns, wondering how far they can go without committing fornication. Should we kiss? Can we engage in heavy petting? Is anything acceptable as long as we don't have intercourse? The Bible doesn't address these questions in detail for unmarried people because there was no such a thing as "dating" in biblical times. Parents usually arranged marriages for their children, and sometimes the children hadn't even met before the wedding was formalized. Opportunities for premarital hanky-panky were few—and if hanky-panky occurred, you were considered as good as married.

Today, with young people delaying marriage for careers, putting more emphasis on romance, and with a general relaxation of morality, dating standards of behavior are very much at issue. While unmarried people don't face the question of sinning against a spouse, they do face the issue of sinning against their own bodies. Engaging in premarital sex is likely to violate the standard that God has established—that sexuality is designed to strengthen the bonds of intimacy between two people who will spend the rest of their lives together.

But, married people sometimes struggle with the question, "How far can I go?" just as unmarried people do. For instance, someone might wonder, "If I dance with a woman who isn't my wife, do I commit adultery?" Or, "If I hold hands with a man who isn't my husband, am I guilty before God?" In effect they're asking, "Where do I draw the line?"—or, to put it another way, "How much can I get away with?" Establishing personal definitions for adultery can be a means of self-justification. "As long as we don't take our clothes off," someone might say to him or herself, "we're not really committing adultery." Several years ago the media frenetically reported the downfall of a famous television evangelist. The stories alleged that the evangelist took prostitutes to hotel rooms and watched them engage in various sex acts. The evangelist swore that he didn't commit adultery, and in the strictest technical sense, that may well be true. But to Jesus, conceiving the act in the mind makes one as liable as performing the act with the body.

This example was an extreme case—most Christians would never take part in such behavior. Emotional adultery can take more innocent forms, as well. I once knew a married man who would greet female friends at parties with a hearty kiss on the lips. His kiss was likely not the "holy kiss" that Paul writes about so often in the New Testament. Perhaps such kissing was normal in the household in which he grew up and meant nothing to him at all. Or perhaps the man took illicit pleasure in sneaking a kiss from a woman other than his wife in a socially acceptable setting. According to Jesus, the legitimacy of his actions would depend on the man's mind-set. If he was attempting to get some measure of sexual gratification out of his stolen kisses, then he was compromising the exclusivity of his relationship with his wife and taking a little stroll down "Adultery Alley."

Another common example of treading too closely to adultery is the exchange of flirtatious remarks with friends or coworkers of the opposite sex. "Heeey, I like the way that sweater fits!" "John, if Nancy ever throws you out of the house, you know who's door you can knock on." If based upon sexual feelings—and not just playfulness and a lack of discretion—such remarks are symptoms of emotional adultery (and grounds for sexual harassment!).

Jesus' teaching also helps us to understand what is *not* adultery. In the Jewish Talmud, there's a hypothetical story wherein the rabbis consider this scenario: A workman is repairing the roof of a house while the householder's wife sunbathes below. Suddenly, a gust of wind sweeps him from the roof, and he falls on top of the householder's wife. They accidentally had sexual contact. Is the pair guilty of adultery? The rabbis said yes, they were. To the rabbis, adultery was the act, not the intention. But Jesus defines adultery on the basis of the state of our hearts, not the position of our bodies. His principle brings the question of fidelity more in line with other biblical teachings. For instance, if adultery were only a matter of acts performed by the body, then married women who were victims of rape would be guilty of committing adultery. Or to be even more speculative, suppose a hypnotist placed a man in a trance, then suggested to him that an unfamiliar woman was his wife. If the man made love to this stranger, would he be committing adultery? Not according to the New Testament standard.

It could be said, then, that the standards Jesus gives for the institution of marriage are both constraining and liberating—constraining because they *do* set limits on our behavior; liberating because they set us free from the hair-splitting and nit-picking of establishing legal guidelines. According to Jesus, marriage is meant for life. Anything that dissolves that relationship, such as divorce, is a deviation from God's original plan. Anything that undermines the integrity of that relationship—whether it's actual adultery or mental unfaithfulness—is sinful as well. Faithfulness to our spouses isn't just a matter of keeping our hands to ourselves. It is also a matter of keeping our thoughts pure and unadulterated by misplaced desires.

A CLEAN MIND

"But," one might well say, "keeping my thoughts pure is easier said than done!" In a society like ours, where we are bombarded with sexual images daily, almost hourly, can we ever really hope to keep our minds pure? Magazines and billboards use sexual imagery to sell everything from alcohol to zoo attractions. Television and radio are cesspools of suggestive comments and titillating situations. Constantly, we're promised that sexual fulfillment will be found somewhere outside the boundaries of marriage. Variety is the spice of life. Forbidden fruit is the sweetest. How can we hope to be pure when our minds are under constant attack? How can we hope to be clean when we live in a pigsty?

First, bear in mind that just because you live in a pigsty, you don't have to go wallowing in the mud. We can minimize our exposure to the sinful influences around us by avoiding situations where we will be tempted to sin. No doubt that's what Jesus meant by "If your right eye causes you to sin, gouge it out and throw it away. It is better for you to lose one part of your body than for your whole body to be thrown into hell." Jesus' words weren't meant to be taken literally. We don't enter into heaven missing eyes or hands. Thus, these words must be understood figuratively—we must remove anything from our lives that causes us to stumble into sin. Even those things that are dear and precious to us should be accounted as rubbish in comparison to the reward of a pure mind. The process of purification can be painful—but the payback is priceless.

The sources of temptation are different for different people. Our libidos are geared differently, so it's impossible for us to set hard and fast guidelines for all people. In general, men are tempted by what they see, while women are tempted more by what they hear or read. Most women would find an intelligent, sympathetic man more sexually attractive than a beefcake in briefs. Most men would find a *Playboy* centerfold more arousing than an impressive résumé. We need to set guidelines for ourselves, based on our own reactions to different situations. If we can't watch television without being tempted to lust, then for—literally—heaven's sake, we should get rid of the television. If we can't go to the beach without falling into sin, then for heaven's sake, we should get our tan somewhere else. If we can't read certain magazines without fantasizing over the situations in the articles or the models in the advertisements, then for heaven's sake, we should cancel our subscriptions.

Like a smoker who's trying to kick the habit, we should avoid the places, people, and situations that subject us to the greatest temptations. Eventually we might reach a point where we are no longer affected by certain temptations. The fact is, sexual temptation in general tends to lose much of its grip as we grow older. But until we're sure that we're safe, we should steer clear of difficult situations. We don't prove how strong we are by putting ourselves in the face of temptation and gritting our teeth. We only prove how foolish we can be. Remember, Paul warned us to *flee* from sexual immorality (1 Cor. 6:18), not stare it down.

It's also helpful to make oneself accountable to another person. Accountability is encouraged by Alcoholics Anonymous as a help to people who struggle with alcohol addiction. We can use the same technique when we're dealing with sexual temptation. It's more difficult to get into trouble when giving regular reports on one's activities to another Christian brother or sister. When feeling especially vulnerable in the face of temptation, before it becomes overwhelming, we should have someone we can call—someone who will say, "Let's pray about this," or, "How about if we go out for a cup of coffee?" It's also good to have Christian colleagues at the office who can hold us accountable for the words we say and the way we say them. Our Christian communities can help us stay out of trouble.

One line of the Lord's Prayer says, "Lead us not into temptation, but deliver us from evil" (Matt. 6:13 KJV). God has given us spiritual and physical resources to avoid temptation. They include the power of the Holy Spirit, our Christian brothers and sisters, and the ability simply to walk away from dangerous situations.

As we strive for purity in today's society, we should bear in mind that just because we can't always avoid temptation doesn't mean that we have to give in to it. Martin Luther said, "You can't stop the birds from flying over your head, but you don't have to let them build a nest in your hair." We are not always going to be free from sexual thoughts or impulses. We won't always be able to avoid feelings of desire for people who aren't our spouses. But we don't have to dwell on these feelings. Again, it's not the flash of emotions that constitutes lust, it's dwelling on it—making the decision to entertain such thoughts. That's when we commit adultery in our hearts. And adultery in our hearts can often lead to adultery with our bodies as well.

Sometimes the temptations come not only from society, but also from our own pasts, and we can't always stop the sinful thoughts from occurring. There's a Devil out there with your name on his manila folder, and he knows where to hit you. We all carry around baggage from our childhoods that can be opened up by the most innocent of cues. I counseled a person once who, when he was a boy, had looked at hard-core pornographic magazines at a friend's house. He had completely forgotten about the incidents until he got seriously involved with a young woman. When he was with her, he sometimes found those forgotten images suddenly popping back to mind. His earliest sexual experiences were being reactivated by his mature, romantic relationship. He was distressed, but I assured him that he wasn't helpless. The birds were flying over his head, but he didn't have to let them build a nest. He could try not to dwell on these thoughts, he could pray about them and trust the grace of God to help him overcome them completely. If a muscle-bound bruiser walks up to you on the street and knocks you to the ground, it's probably best not to jump up and engage him in a fistfight. Let the police handle him. Likewise, trying to overcome temptation by an act of your will is not a wise strategy. Turn the matter over to the Holy Spirit and put yourself out of harm's way.

Sexual feelings can be powerful, almost overwhelming at times. We can't always ignore them, but we don't need to dwell on them. Go for a bike ride. Play a game with your children. Call your mother on the phone. Watch an Abbott and Costello movie. Go serve soup at a homeless shelter. Sex is good, but there's so much more to life than sex. The more fully we're engaged in all of life, the less power sexual temptation has over us.

ADULTERY, IN SUMMARY

The commandment against adultery was originally understood by the Israelites as a protection of the family property. But that's not what God had in mind. God designed marriage so that we can be known and accepted by another human being. Marriage is meant to be a relationship in which we can be vulnerable and open, yet unafraid and unashamed. Sex is a part of that grand design. It requires us to be vulnerable and makes us even more vulnerable in the process. Acting out our sexuality with a person other than a spouse breaks down the integrity of the marriage relationship.

Faithfulness to our spouses begins in our hearts. We can't enjoy fantasies about other people and still maintain the bond of openness and trust that God wants in our marriages. So the secret to marital fidelity is a pure heart and a clean mind. If lustful thoughts are not allowed to reside in the mind, they'll never be acted out in the body.

QUESTIONS FOR REFLECTION

1. Compare some contemporary TV marriages to some classic depictions. How do they differ? Which do you feel are more realistic?
2. How has the popular media influenced your perceptions of the opposite sex? Of your own sex?
3. How self-consistent was the ancient Israelite view of marriage and adultery? Do you think similar ideas continue in modern society?
4. How does adultery break down the intimacy in a marital

relationship? Do you think we can trust people who cheat on their spouses?

5. Do you think there's such a thing as harmless sexual fantasy? When is fantasy harmful?

t e n

Theft and Stewardship

You shall not steal.
—Exodus 20:15

WITH THE EIGHTH COMMANDMENT, the Ten Commandments continue the progression that we've already observed. The first four dealt with our relationship to God and creation. Then we received a command concerning respect for our parents that served as a "bridge" to principles governing human relations. Next, we were given instruction regarding the sanctity of human life. After that, we were given a command about the most significant human relationship, the relationship between a married couple. The eighth commandment shifts from the realm of personal injury to matters of property.

It's also clear that the commandments progress from the more serious sins to the less serious. If a man steals from his neighbor, he does less damage than if he slept with his wife—and far less damage than if he killed him. The prohibition of theft doesn't carry the same kind of urgency as do the earlier commandments. That's not to say that the eighth commandment is less important, or that God is willing to wink at thieves. But there is no doubt that some sins are worse than others. The pious-sounding adage that "sin is sin is sin," and all sin is the same in God's eyes, contains a measure of truth, but only a little. True, any sin separates us from God; and yes, a thief is just as deeply in need of God's grace as a murderer is. But ask the man who was mugged for his wallet if he'd rather his attacker had shot him dead. Ask the woman whose car was stolen if she'd rather that her husband committed adultery. Obviously, some sins do more damage than other sins. God is very much concerned when we injure each other—the deeper the injury, the greater his concern. God's judgment will fall more harshly on those who commit the greater sins.

In some cultures, the severity of theft was judged on the basis of whom you stole from. Under ancient Assyrian law, if you stole from a nobleman, your hand would be cut off. Stealing from people of lower classes, however, carried lighter penalties. Recently in England, an Anglican clergyman tried to reverse the ancient standard. According to the Associated Press, Rev. John Papworth told BBC Radio that stealing from large corporations was acceptable, while stealing from individuals or small merchants was wrong. Big corporations, Papworth reasoned, are hurting small businesses and communities, so they deserve whatever ill-treatment they receive at the hands of thieves.

The Ten Commandments do not make distinctions between class and affluence. The eighth commandment, like the sixth and the seventh, is wonderfully terse—just two words in Hebrew: Don't steal. In God's view, the question isn't from whom you are stealing or why you are stealing. The principle is that stealing is simply wrong. But while we may believe we know what stealing is, it'll take a little biblical investigation to determine what exactly the Bible considers stealing and why God prohibits it.

HOW DARE THEY!

My first adult encounter with theft came shortly after my wife and I moved to Chicago for graduate school. We had lived in the neighborhood for perhaps three weeks when someone broke into our little car and stole the stereo out of the dash. Needless to say, I was angry. As a student, I didn't have a lot of money to throw around, and that stereo represented something of a splurge on my part. As I talked to a neighbor about the experience, she said, "Isn't it terrible? You feel so violated." Actually, I didn't feel particularly violated. I just wanted my stereo back.

A few months later, my hapless automobile was once again the target of sticky fingers. This time, the hubcaps were stolen. I drove without hubcaps for a while, but with winter coming on, I decided my wheels needed some protection against Chicago road salt. I bought a cheap set of replacement hubcaps. In a few weeks, they were stolen as well.

What's wrong with people? Don't they realize that stealing is wrong? I was amazed that people could take such a cavalier attitude toward the property of others. Disregard for others' rights of ownership, however, is a pretty common attitude. Several years ago in Detroit, a man made the headlines when he shot and killed a teenager who was trying to steal his hubcaps. I myself couldn't imagine killing someone over something so trivial, but I was amazed at the attitude of local political and religious figures. They expressed full support when the boy's mother said, "He wasn't doing anything wrong! He was just stealing hubcaps!" True, stealing hubcaps is hardly a capital offense, but how can anyone say with a straight face that the youth didn't do anything wrong? He made off with someone else's hubcaps!

Even clergy can be subject to the sticky-finger syndrome. A clerk in a Christian bookstore told me about an incident where a well-known minister in town had come into the store, selected a stack of Christian albums, and walked out the door without paying. When he was caught later, he indignantly claimed that he had a right to take the albums since he was using them for the Lord's work. I asked the clerk if such incidents were common, and he said yes—they especially had to watch ministers very closely when they came "shopping."

Apparently, human beings have no biological drive that compels us to respect the property of others. Any one of us might become a thief, albeit the circumstances would have to be severe for most of us to commit larceny. Yet, all humans have some innate concept of private property. One of the first words most children learn is "Mine!" Thus the potential for conflict is ripe. On the one hand, we want to keep what is ours, while on the other hand, some people want to take what belongs to someone else.

SHOULD WE HAVE PRIVATE PROPERTY?

The notion of private property is the very basis for the prohibition against stealing. You can't steal from someone if no one owns anything. If we could eliminate the need to *own* things, then stealing wouldn't be a problem. In his song "Imagine," John Lennon captured the thoughts of millions when he invited us to envision a world without private property. The lyrics ask us to imagine a world with no possessions, where there is no need for greed or hunger, where all the people share all the world. It sounds like a dreamy utopia. Of course, there'd be no stealing in such a world, since no one has any private claims on property. The need for the eighth commandment would be eliminated.

The limited efforts that have been made to do away with private property, however, have been a dismal failure. Karl Marx predicted the creation of a classless society, where the notion of personal ownership would be essentially abolished. In Marx's vision, all goods would be owned and distributed by the community, so there'd be no chance of anyone becoming rich at the expense of others. Nikolai Lenin tried to found the Soviet Union on Marx's communist ideals. Contrary to Marx, however, the Russians never completely did away with private ownership. Even this circumscribed attempt at "sharing the wealth" has proven a failure, as the history books show.

Communist states might look good in theory, but they can't overcome the problem of human nature. Basically, we're greedy. We like the idea of accumulating wealth, even at the expense of others. We also like tangible rewards for our achievements. People are disinclined to do their best work if not motivated by the promise of a bigger paycheck. And so, even communist states discovered that they couldn't do away with the notion of private ownership. Two generations of "education" in the Soviet Union and Communist China couldn't eradicate the human desire for personal acquisition.

Other attempts have been made to do away with private property. In the United States, idealistic people formed communes where they could live together, share the work, and share the wealth. The *kibbutzim*, the communal farms in Israel, are another example of an experiment in shared living. But such ideal communities seem to attract only the young and the dreamers. And, even so, a commune where everyone shared the same clothes is unheard of. It seems that the only way to completely do away with private ownership would be to change human nature. If we were all so selfless that we could work for the common good with no expectation of reward, then the system of communism might work. But, alas, we're a fallen race, born with innate self-interest that in this world we will never completely overcome.

Even Christians aren't immune to the effects of sin. In the New Testament, Luke writes wistfully about the community of Christians in Jerusalem. These believers held all things in common, claiming no exclusive ownership of any goods, and they freely shared with anyone in need (Acts 2:44-47). Yet, when Luke writes his account in the latter half of the first century, it sounds like he's describing a system that no longer existed. When the early believers lived in close communion with each other and the Holy Spirit, they could share all things in common. But as the Spirit became less prominent in their lives, the system collapsed as well.

Even in the earliest days, there were problems with the "all things in common" principle. In Acts 5:1-11, Luke writes about a couple named Ananias and Sapphira who sold some property, brought part of the proceeds to the disciples, and told the community that they'd given all their wealth to be shared among the believers. Peter reproved them for their treachery, telling them that the property and the proceeds from its sale were theirs to do with as they pleased. They weren't under any compulsion to give the money to the church. They had sinned, however, in attempting to deceive the church and the Holy Spirit. The couple died on the spot—the story doesn't tell us whether they were slain by God or simply victims of heart attacks.

This episode tells us two things about the concept of private property. First, there is no divine mandate to give up private property in favor of communal living. While it sounds like a nice system, God doesn't require us to live in such a fashion. Second, even in the best possible earthly situation, humans are still human. Even with the mighty aid of the Holy Spirit, we can't completely overcome our human natures. God recognizes our weaknesses and makes concessions for them.

GOD'S VIEW OF PRIVATE PROPERTY

So, we must make a distinction between the ideal situation and the real world in which we live. True, there'd be no reason to steal—and thus no need for a prohibition against stealing—if everything was held as common property. Perhaps communal living would ultimately be the best situation for all of us. In heaven, I doubt that there will be much concern about setting apart one person's goods from another's. But we're not there yet. And until we get there, we have to live in a world where my things are mine, and yours are yours, and we must respect that arrangement.

One shouldn't make the mistake, however, of assuming that God's view of possessions is the same as ours. God accommodates our understanding of private property, maybe even encourages it, but adds a condition. We can claim exclusive *use* of certain items or objects. God has no quarrel with that. Claiming that we *own* things, however, is a different matter. According to the Bible, God is the ultimate owner of all things in heaven and earth: "For every animal of the forest is mine, and the cattle on a thousand hills. . . . For the world is mine, and all that is in it" (Ps. 50:10, 12b; see also Deut. 10:14). In fact, one of God's titles in the Old Testament, *Qoneh Shamayim wa'Aretz,* means "Possessor of Heaven and Earth" (Gen. 14:19, 22). We may be allowed exclusive use of some things, but in the end, all things are God's. While from the human perspective we are the owners of property, God views us as stewards of the things that he has entrusted to us. He has established certain mechanisms through which his property is distributed among human beings, work, for instance, or inheritance. But ultimately, God is sovereign over all that he places in our care.

The Old Testament provides an excellent example of God's sovereign ownership and human stewardship in the teaching concerning land. God gives the land of Canaan to the Canaanites for a time. But because of their wickedness, God takes the land away from them and gives it to Abraham and his descendants (Gen. 13:14-17; 15:18-21; Lev. 18:25). If the Israelites prove to be unworthy, God threatens to take the land away from them as well (Deut. 28:58-63; 30:17-18;

2 Kings 17:1-23). God gives the land to the different nations, but it's only theirs so long as God says so.

Individuals, too, can own land only at God's decree. At the time of the conquest of Canaan, each Israelite family was given an inheritance of land that was to be theirs perpetually. They could sell the land, but at the end of forty-nine years, in the year of Jubilee ("the blowing of the trumpet"), the land would revert back to its original owners (Lev. 25:8-55). Through this system, God sought to insure that no one could become permanently dispossessed, and no one could become excessively wealthy. Theoretically, there'd be no lower class living through generations of poverty. So, even though God gave the land to the various families, he still determined how they could use it.

A similar principle of stewardship is present in the teaching about tithes. In the Old Testament, the Israelites were required to give ten percent of their produce or income to the support of the temple and priesthood (Lev. 27:30; Num. 18:21-24). Giving the tithe did not discharge one's entire duty to God. Rather, the tithe had a symbolic significance. If God required that ten percent of an Israelite's income was to be used in a certain way, then it implied that he had lordship over all of the Israelite's possessions. Those who failed to pay the tithe were regarded as thieves—not just because they were stealing God's ten percent, but because they were taking advantage of God's generosity (Mal. 3:6-12).

To clarify, consider the following hypothetical situation: Marcia allows her sister-in-law Amy to use her duplex for a few months. All Marcia asks in return is that Amy mow the lawn every week. A couple of weeks go by, the grass gets tall, and the neighbors call Marcia to complain. Marcia calls Amy, and Amy explains that she's been busy, but she'll get around to mowing the grass soon. A month goes by, and the yard looks like a nature preserve. If Amy consistently fails to mow the lawn, eventually Marcia's going to get angry, not so much because Amy's cheating Marcia in regard to the chore, but because she's taking advantage of Marcia's property and generosity. Essentially, Amy's stealing the use of the duplex. Likewise, the Israelites who failed to tithe weren't cheating God out of "his" 10 percent—they were stealing all of their property from God by failing to fulfill their end of the bargain. They did not appreciate that they were living off of God's gifts.

In the New Testament, the principles of stewardship are taught even more clearly. In the parable of the talents, Jesus tells us that God will hold us accountable for our use of the things that he has placed in our care (Matt. 25:14-30). Paul tells Timothy to warn rich people not to hope in their riches but to hope in God, who provides all things for our enjoyment. Paul writes that Timothy should order the rich to share freely with anyone in need (1 Tim. 6:17-18). Elsewhere, we read that our very lives and bodies are not our own. They belong to Jesus Christ to be used as he sees fit (Rom. 12:1; 1 Cor. 6:19-20).

One might well say, "Now wait a minute. I've worked hard for what I've got. I put myself through college and graduate school flipping hamburgers and scrubbing toilets. I put in long hours to work my way up the ladder of success. And you're telling me that everything I've earned isn't mine to do with as I see fit?" It does seem a bit presumptuous. Yet looking at the bigger picture, we recognize the flimsiness of our claim to have earned our possessions. One doesn't choose one's biological makeup. If a person is more talented, smarter, or better-looking than average, that person can thank God for the genetic gift that made him or her that way. None of us chose our families. If we had the privilege of being born into a wealthy family or a household that encouraged hard work and education, we should thank God for a blessing that many people in this world never receive. We didn't choose the country in which we were born. In many parts of the world, children hardly have the opportunity to grow up, let alone go to school or college. I'm convinced that no one ever became a success without a "lucky break" here or there, an unmerited and unexpected blessing that opened doors of opportunity. So, in substantial measure, the difference between the rich person and the poor person is the grace of God. Yes, we might have made some profitable decisions along the way, but it was only because of God's grace that we had any choice at all.

Thus, we haven't a right to claim anything for ourselves. All of our "private property" is really on loan from God. Ownership is an illusion, and the Lord who gives may collect his property any time he sees fit, as he did from Job (Job 1:21). We should develop an attitude toward our possessions like the attitude of the apostle Paul: learn to be happy with much or learn to be happy with little (Phil. 4:11–13). God gives us what he deems best.

STEALING AS A SIN AGAINST GOD

If I've given my car "on loan" to a friend and someone steals it from him, I am ultimately the injured party. When we think of our possessions as things "on loan" from God, it puts a different light on stealing. Stealing isn't just an insult to the theft victim—it's an insult to God. If God has granted a woman a piece of property and an unscrupulous developer swindles her out of it, the swindler has then overthrown God's will. The matter of overturning God's will is part of the reason why he becomes so angry in the Old Testament about people who plunder and oppress the poor (Isa. 3:14; Amos 2:7; 4:1). It's not that God loves poor people more than he loves rich people. And heaven knows that poverty doesn't necessarily make a person righteous. But God has willed that everyone should have an equal opportunity to enjoy the fruit of their labor. Those who oppress the poor and accumulate wealth at the expense of others demonstrate a disdain for God's will.

This fact illustrates something significant about the nature of sin: all sin, in a sense, is sin against God. Modern society tends to define sin, if it thinks of sin at all, as actions that hurt other people. Most secular people don't consider idolatry or heresy or taking God's name in vain as sins. Such behaviors, they reason, don't hurt anybody. Isn't God too big and too loving to be petty about such things? But when we look at the Bible, we find that all sin involves an element of insult to God. Disrespect for one's parents is sinful because parents are an earthly manifestation of the divine hierarchy. Murder is sinful because it's a blow against God's image on earth. Adultery is sinful because it undermines God's purpose for marriage. All that doesn't mean that God isn't concerned about what we do to each other. But, in the final analysis, the way we treat each other is ultimately of less consequence to our eternal well-being than is our attitude toward God.

The second greatest commandment, says Jesus, is to love our neighbors, but the greatest commandment is to love God (Matt. 22:36–40; Mark 12:28–31). It is a sin if we hate our neighbors, but, more important, hate betrays a lack of love for God, because our neighbors are made in his image (1 John 4:20).

The sin of theft is partly its injury to the victim, but the greater sin is that it's an insult to God. It is a violation against his image (in our neighbors) and an attempt to thwart his will. God wants human beings to know the dignity of enjoying the fruit of their labors. When others frustrate that plan, they are not only injuring their neighbor—they are working against the will of God.

Someone might try to justify theft by arguing that God can use thieves to accomplish his various purposes. If, for instance, the Lord gives, and the Lord takes away, he can surely use a swindler to redistribute wealth. And the Bible also contains examples of God using thieves as a disciplinary tool. During the days of the judges God used brigands to oppress the Israelites and lead them to repentance.

There *is* a grain of truth in this logic. God certainly uses sinners, and even sin itself, to accomplish good in the world. A clear example of this principle in the Old Testament is in the story of Joseph. He was kidnapped and sold into slavery by his brothers, and yet God used this act of treachery to preserve the Israelite race (Gen. 37; 39–45). And no act was more sinful, and more beneficial, than the crucifixion of Jesus. If God didn't use sin and sinners, he'd have precious little to work with! Yet the fact that God can produce good results from sinful acts does not make the sin less wicked. We fall deeply into error when we justify injustice and inequities in terms of "God's will." It is *not* God's will that people suffer and starve because of human sins. To claim so is to say that God is the author of sin, a charge perilously close to blasphemy. Yes, there are cases in which God uses theft. There might be times when God *wants* to take someone's possessions away and uses a thief to accomplish that end. But we don't have insight into the mind of God to discern those situations, and we certainly haven't leave to accomplish God's will through theft. God will not command us to steal or to do anything that contradicts his will as revealed in the Scriptures. Thieves have no part in God's kingdom (1 Cor. 6:10).

DEGREES OF THEFT

To better understand the purposes behind the Ten Commandments, in most of the previous chapters we've worked from specific examples of sins to arrive at a general principle. This chapter works in reverse, from the principle to the specifics. So far, we've determined that God is concerned about our property rights, that God regards us as stewards of his property rather than owners who can do whatever we please with our possessions, and that those who steal from others insult God. But what does God consider to be stealing? How does God define an act of theft?

Some Bible scholars argue that the eighth commandment does not refer to theft in general, but only to kidnapping. The Hebrew verb used in this verse, which I've translated "steal," can refer both to stealing objects and to stealing people—that is, kidnapping, whether for ransom or to make someone a slave (see Exod. 21:16; Deut. 24:7; which use the same verb). Kidnapping, like murder and adultery, was a capital offense under biblical law. Theft, however, was not. The thief was simply required to make restitution and pay a penalty. Some scholars argue that since the first seven commandments all cover crimes punishable by death, this eighth commandment must refer to a capital offense as well—hence, kidnapping. But there's no reason to conclude that the eighth commandment is in the same "class" as the preceding commandments. Rather, the commandments are progressing in order from more serious to less serious. The eighth commandment falls into the less serious end of the spectrum—although not yet as minor as the tenth commandment, which prohibits even the desire for someone else's property.

So, I believe the eighth commandment should be understood broadly to mean theft of either persons or property. It covers a spectrum of sins, the most severe of which would be stealing people. Kidnapping deprives someone of his or her freedom, usually with the threat of force, even deadly force. This crime, like murder, is an attack on the personhood of someone made in God's image. Individuals, made in the image of God, have a right to life, freedom, and dignity—unless, through their own sin, they forfeit that right. Anyone who violates those rights is insulting God's image on earth. (As the implications of this understanding of human worth became increasingly clear, it eventually led to the abolition of slavery in Europe and America.) As in the case of murder, then, the penalty for kidnapping was death (Exod. 21:16; Deut. 24:7).

Property theft can also be categorized into degrees of severity. In our own legal system, we distinguish between the thief who threatens others and forces them to turn over their property, and the one who breaks into a house and sneaks away with the goods. The first case is considered much worse, since it implies the use of deadly force. Someone who uses a gun or knife in a robbery can expect, if caught, to spend several years in prison.

The Bible, too, makes the distinction of force. In Scripture, criminals who used force or coercion to deprive others of their property are usually called "oppressors." The biblical law code has surprisingly little to say about them, except perhaps for a brief mention in Leviticus 6:1-5, which requires that anyone who through oppression deprives another of property must make restitution for what was stolen and must pay a fine. But even in the Leviticus passage, the reference clearly isn't to a criminal who threatens to club his neighbor to death if he doesn't surrender his money. Instead, it has much less severe threats in mind—perhaps threats of legal action or swindling. The ruffians who use the threat of violence to steal from others are not mentioned in the Law, but the Prophets and some other Old Testament writings speak often of them. Usually, they're grouped together with murderers and other wicked folks (e.g., Jer. 22:17; Ezek. 22:12; Hab. 2:6-8). Often, they preyed on the poor and widows—people who didn't have the resources to defend themselves against such bullies (Prov. 22:16; Ezek. 18:12; Amos 4:1). Just like the murderer and the kidnapper, the oppressor demonstrates a lack of discernment of God's image on earth: "He who oppresses the poor shows contempt for their Maker" (Prov. 14:31a).

While oppressors were considered vile fellows, thieves were regarded more as nuisances. Most discussions of theft in the Law seem to have a nonviolent crime in mind. The thief wasn't someone who held a weapon over you and demanded your money, but rather someone who slipped into your pasture and carried off some of your sheep. In part, the Old Testament understanding of theft as a nonviolent act arises from the state of society in those days. You couldn't go to the corner pawnshop and buy a gun. Also, if you had enough money to buy a sword, considering the cost of metal in those days, you generally didn't need to steal. So, the average thief wouldn't have been well armed and ready for a fight. In fact, the Law is more concerned about a homeowner killing a thief than a thief killing a homeowner. According to Exodus 22:1-2, if a homeowner surprised a thief and killed him during the night, the homeowner wasn't liable to prosecution. But if a homeowner killed a thief during the day—when the thief could have been avoided, or the homeowner could have called for help or subdued the thief with less chance of injury—the homeowner was liable to prosecution as a murderer!

That's not to say that theft was excused. The Law contains a number of discussions covering different kinds of theft, from a simple, "He snuck in the back door and carried off everything he could get his hands on" (see Exod. 22:1) to a more complicated, "I found Bob's heifer wandering by the road and she followed me home. Now, if that heifer calls Bob on the phone, he can have her back" (see Lev. 6:3). In the Bible, both cases are treated the same. Property that belongs to someone else has been stolen. The thief must return the property, pay a fine to the property owner, and make a sacrifice to the Lord (Lev. 6:5-7). A thief who had no money was sold as a slave so that restitution could be made (Exod. 22:3). When the Bible commands that an Israelite be sold as a slave, the crime is clearly considered a serious one.

THE MODERN CHRISTIAN THIEF

Most Christians aren't tempted to such overt acts of theft. If they do succumb, they feel a sense of guilt—unless, apparently, they are pastors doing a little Christian bookstore shopping. And despite Rev. Papworth's argument—that stealing from big and impersonal chain stores is justifiable—it's hard to imagine any Christian feeling justified to walk into a Wal-Mart and lift items from the shelves. As the retailers quickly remind us, such theft doesn't just hurt the store, it hurts the consumers as well. Consumers, through higher prices, pay for the stolen items and for the expensive security measures that stores take to protect their goods. Even if one argues that the big stores exploit consumers and deserve to be "ripped off," the thieves do far more harm to their neighbors than they do to the store's board of directors.

So, it's easy for us to see the shoplifter as a thief. But there are other, less blatant, ways to steal from a large corporation. Making copies of computer programs, videotapes, or CDs is stealing in much the same way as shoplifting. People often justify such theft by arguing, "If the company charged fair prices for this software [or tape, or whatever], I wouldn't be forced to make a copy for my own use." The rationalization is similar to Rev. Papworth's argument: They aren't hurting some poor individual or small company. In fact, they can almost view their theft as a just, grand crusade. Even Robin Hood-esque!

As in the case of a shoplifter, the software or video pirate is actually doing more harm to his or her fellow consumers than to the media company. The basic flaw in rationalizing such sin, however, is that it places part of the blame for the sin on the victims. This rationale does not view acts as right or wrong in themselves, but only right or wrong in light of the character of the person who is injured by them. Could you imagine if such reasoning were applied to other sins? The rapist wasn't really sinning, because the woman he attacked wasn't a virgin. The murderer wasn't at fault, because the man he stalked and killed was a liar. The adulterer was innocent, because his wife was a shrew.

Some crimes may be worse when the victims are especially innocent. We are more outraged when someone robs a poor widow than when someone robs a rich slumlord. But theft cannot be justified because the victim was evil. Even if a man steals from big companies that overcharge, use deceptive practices, or drive smaller companies out of business, he's still a thief. Stealing from the poor makes the sin even worse, but stealing from the rich doesn't make the sin righteous.

WORKPLACE LARCENY

As we've seen, theft is not just a crime against individuals. It can also be perpetrated against businesses and corporations. But slumlords and deceptive business people are not just victims of theft; they can be victimizers as well. There are certainly swindlers out in the business world. And swindlers are thieves—even "oppressors," to use the biblical term. Just like the man who breaks into your home and carries off your silverware, the swindler takes your money or property without due recompense. Thus, the car dealer who knowingly sells a "lemon" for twice its value and a slum lord who uses threats against his tenants to extract high rent for substandard housing are both thieves.

More common than these disreputable characters are the workplace thieves. These people take home pencils from the office, tools from the shop, or copy software from the office computer. Perhaps they think workers deserve to take a few things home. They work hard for the company, they argue, and they should have a share of the profits. A big company will never miss a few pencils. Like the Robin Hood types, these thieves justify the sin by concentrating on the nature of the victim. Surely it's all right to steal a few items here and there from a big company with lots of resources. But God, who owns all things, was concerned that the Israelites were stealing tithes from his storehouses. God was not impoverished by such stealing, but he deplored the attitude that such petty theft represented—disrespect for God and lack of discernment of his lordship. Likewise, when an employee takes home a few pencils from the office, the thievery may not do great damage to the business, but the thief certainly betrays his or her selfishness and lack of appreciation for the company that puts food on the table. The company might easily absorb the losses, but the thief can't so easily escape the guilt.

Lest I make God sound pro big business, let me add another example of theft, one that the Bible views in a particularly harsh light. Employers who take advantage of their workers, refusing to pay them a fair wage, are called "oppressors"—the violent kind of thieves mentioned in Malachi 3:5. The Bible groups them together with sorcerers, adulterers, and other particularly bad sinners. Exploitative employers make use of the strengths and abilities of their employees without giving them a fair exchange, which is the basic definition of a thief. Jesus, and Paul too, tell us that the laborer is worthy of his hire (Luke 10:7; 1 Tim. 5:18). Workers deserve their rewards.

Why does God take a harsh stand against such employers? It's because God created human beings to work and to enjoy the fruit of their labors (Gen. 2:15-16; 3:19). When workers can't enjoy the fruit, their work loses some of its intrinsic dignity, and so do the workers. They can't experience the pride of creating—one of the human abilities that reflects the image of God in us. One of the tragedies of industrialization is that it inserts several degrees of separation between laborers and the products they produce. Workers on an assembly line usually don't produce a finished product that they can use or sell. They are responsible for only a small part of a product, a product they might not even be able to afford. So workers may experience a sense of pointlessness and futility about their labor.

This sense of futility might well contribute to another kind of theft—the worker who doesn't put in a fair day's work. Between high school and college, I worked for a summer in a factory. Soon after I started, one of the workers took me under his wing and showed me the ropes: "Here's where you hide when you want to take a break—the supervisors never come back here! You really want to get assigned to that machine there. The quota's so low on it you don't have to do anything all day!" People who take a paycheck for work they haven't done are thieves, just as companies that oppress their workers are thieves. God has given us jobs through our employers in order to provide for our needs, but also that we might be productive. In the parable of the talents (Matt. 25:14-30), Jesus had strong words about an employee who failed to do his job. The employees who did their work conscientiously were rewarded with greater responsibility and blessings. The one who was lazy was cast into the outer darkness.

God values our work, even if we live in a society that sometimes devalues it. He expects us to do it well, to treat our employers and employees with respect, giving honest wages for honest work. Those who do otherwise are thieves. Paul encourages us, "He who has been stealing must steal no longer, but must work, doing something useful with his own hands, that he may have something to share with those in need" (Eph. 4:28). It's a strong admonition that applies not only to people who skulk around in alleys looking for something to filch.

It applies, as well, to the worker who is hoping the boss won't catch him asleep at his desk.

IS STEALING EVER JUSTIFIED?

A favorite pastime for ethicists is to find loopholes in the laws. Is it always wrong to steal, they ask? Are there ever conditions where stealing is justified, even righteous? And in fact, there may be cases where taking something that doesn't belong to you is the "right" thing to do. For instance, the Bible tells us that when King Ahaziah of Judah died, his mother, Athaliah, tried to kill off all heirs to the throne to take the throne for herself. But a princess named Jehosheba literally "stole" one of Ahaziah's sons and hid him from his grandmother until he came of age (2 Chron. 22:11). In this case, stealing was an act of mercy that prevented a murder. In this instance, it obviously wasn't wrong to steal.

It will only lead to trouble, however, if we start thinking in terms of the end justifying the means—that a good outcome makes it okay to sin. In the above example, we're mistaken if we conclude that Jehosheba's "sin" was justified solely because it prevented a murder. Rather, we must recognize that in this case, stealing wasn't a sin. In our Christian understanding, sin isn't defined by the act, but by the motivation behind the act. Those who steal for the purpose of depriving others of rightful property and making it their own have sinned. A man who takes bread to feed his starving children has sinned—though I imagine that God and the courts would be mercifully in such a case. Yet it is unlikely that a person who steals a detonator from a nuclear bomb that is set to explode under the United Nations building would be considered a sinner. In this case, the person who steals the detonator isn't seeking to derive benefit for himself by depriving someone else of his or her property. He is "stealing" to save people's lives. If I stole a bottle of barbiturates from a suicidal friend, I'm trying to protect her life, not deprive her of property. Again, I wouldn't be guilty of the sin of stealing.

We human beings are very good, however, at deceiving ourselves and convincing ourselves that our motives are good, when in fact they may be less than pure. Note the self-styled Robin Hood types who convince themselves that they're obligated to shoplift from big department stores or to copy video tapes because giant corporations need to be taught a lesson. Such rationalization might be more believable if the thieves didn't derive any benefit from their booty—if, for instance, they actually gave all their ill-gotten gains to the poor. In that case, they're probably motivated by a desire to help the poor rather than to deprive the rich. They would still be guilty of breaking the civil law, as well as exercising poor judgment (since better ways exist to help the poor than by stealing from the wealthy), but I doubt if God would charge them with the sin of stealing. But, I never claim to fully know the mind of God.

It would be easier to discern the moral acceptability of theft if we could develop a one-size-fits-all, ironclad rule for when stealing is justified, but that doesn't seem possible. Under certain extreme circumstances, especially those where life is endangered, stealing may well be appropriate. Such cases, though, are rare. God hasn't given humanity the insight to know which people should be deprived of the property with which God has entrusted them. If God wishes to redistribute the wealth, he has ways of doing so that won't require us to sneak into someone's window at night.

RULES AND PRINCIPLES

The above ethical discussion emphasizes once again that Christians must internalize principles of conduct and not merely set rules for themselves. A large section of this chapter gives some guidelines regarding theft, but those guidelines arise from a basic principle. God has distributed possessions among us according to his will and plan. He has established principles whereby we receive what we need as rewards for our labors, through inheritance, as gifts. We are not to frustrate God's plan by stealing from our neighbors. In essence, the thief is putting himself in the place of God, deciding that he knows how possessions should be distributed.

No doubt, wealth isn't going to all the places where God would like it to go. It is an unfortunate fact that a lot of thieves inhabit the world—people who accumulate wealth, often dishonestly and always at the expense of others. We are sometimes tempted to redistribute the wealth by whatever means necessary. Bloody revolutions have been driven by such a desire. Yet history has shown that more theft won't solve the problem of stealing. We have to trust God's providence and God's justice to balance all accounts—in the end.

QUESTIONS FOR REFLECTION

1. Have you ever been robbed? How did the experience make you feel?
2. Do you think human beings are too attached to possessions? Can you think of ways that we could do away with, or reduce, ownership of private property?
3. Can you imagine any circumstances that might make you resort to theft? Can you think of other possible responses to those circumstances?
4. Do you think our legal system ever prosecutes the victim instead of the perpetrator? Do you find it offensive that the argument of victimization is used to justify theft?
5. Do you think Robin Hood was a sinner? In similar circumstances—faced with an oppressive, autocratic governor robbing the poor—what might you do?

e l e v e n

Words That Wound

You shall not give false testimony against your neighbor.
—Exodus 20:16

NEARING THE END OF THE Ten Commandments, the crimes that are proscribed become ever less severe—at least in human eyes. The ninth commandment moves from the realm of physical injury to verbal injury. The sixth, seventh, and eighth commandments—"You shall not kill"; "You shall not commit adultery"; "You shall not steal"—all address harm that's directed to the victim by the sinner. This one, however, involves a more craven, indirect attack. The efforts of the sinner aren't targeted directly against the victim, but harm is accomplished by way of the victim's community.

To illustrate, think of a person as being surrounded by concentric circles, like a bull's eye. The central circle represents the person him- or herself; the next circle out represents the family circle; the third represents property and possessions; the next, the community in which he or she lives. The sixth commandment, "You shall not kill," outlaws an assault on the central circle, the physical being of the individual. The seventh commandment, "You shall not commit adultery," deals with assault on his or her family circle. The eighth commandment, "You shall not steal," protects the individual from assault on his or her possessions. Each successive commandment addresses a sin that is a little less direct, a little less "fatal." The ninth commandment, however, concerns an attack that isn't directed physically at the victim or the victim's household. Rather, it's an assault on the person's reputation. The damage could ultimately be just as great as if the victim had been murdered, but it's done in an indirect fashion.

Undermining a person's reputation in the community, for instance, can have dire consequences. When I was in my teens, my family experienced a series of devastating crises. My father was a partner in a small engineering firm, but because of a bad economy and some difficult circumstances the business went bankrupt. For nearly a year, Dad pounded the pavement looking for a new position, but he had no luck. Finally, he was hired by a large firm that had heard good things about him. Several months later, my father's boss mentioned to him that they almost hadn't hired him. One of his references had told the company that my father was an unreliable drunkard—a charge that couldn't have been farther from the truth. The only reason the company had taken a chance on my dad was because his record of accomplishments cast doubt on the charge of drunkenness.

The consequences of spreading false testimony can be devastating. How many lives have been ruined by spiteful people who couldn't express their anger or resentment outright? How many church schisms have been caused by a person who didn't have the courage to confront another individual over an issue? By bringing the opinion of the community to bear against a person, the false witness hopes to keep his or her hands clean from inflicting any physical harm. It's likely that most bearers of false testimony convince themselves that they're really innocent of wrongdoing. They just repeat something they heard or something that could have been true. Some people, however, are truly malicious, thinking that starting a false rumor could be the most effective way to destroy their enemies. Often times, they are right. A false rumor can turn the whole community against someone, robbing him or her of reputation, friends, livelihood, even his or her very life. Yes, this sin is an "indirect" attack on one's neighbor, but it is hardly less dangerous than a direct attack. Sometimes the very cravenness of the assault makes it even more wicked.

THE COURTROOM SETTING

What circumstances did God have in mind when issuing this commandment? Most scholars agree that it envisions a courtroom setting. No doubt, the language implies such a situation. The words can be literally translated, "You shall not respond against your neighbor with a false testimony." The phrase "respond against your neighbor" implies the question and answer format used in the courtroom. So if this is indeed the case, a great deal was at stake. Someone on trial for a capital offense, such as murder or adultery, could find him- or herself at the wrong end of a stone if a witness presented false testimony. Someone on trial for a lesser crime or someone appearing before a judge in a civil dispute could be seriously "inconvenienced" if a false testimony was accepted as fact.

Biblical law tried to protect against such abuses. No one could be put to death on the testimony of one witness alone—two or three witnesses were required (Num. 35:30; Deut. 19:15). Even so, witnesses could be bribed, as they were in the case of Naboth. Naboth was a poor man who had the misfortune of owning a vineyard that King Ahab coveted (1 Kings 21). Ahab's queen, Jezebel, hired a couple of rogues to claim that they had heard Naboth curse God and the king. So Naboth was arrested, tried, and executed on the testimony of false witnesses.

Witnesses could also conspire together to give false testimony. In the Apocrypha's story of Susanna (which is found in Daniel 13 in the Roman Catholic version of the Bible), two lustful men tried to blackmail Susanna into committing adultery with them. When she refused, they claimed that they had seen her committing adultery with another man. Daniel examined each of them separately on a detail of their story, and when their two accounts differed, the liars were executed.

As another safeguard against false testimony, the Law of Moses prescribed that whoever issued false testimony would suffer the fate that the testifier had intended for the person slandered (Deut. 19:19). In other words, if you were caught issuing false testimony in a capital trial, your penalty was death. If you gave a false testimony in a civil trial in order to get hold of someone's property, you'd forfeit your own property. Judges in Old Testament times did not mete out a little slap on the wrist. Perjurers received the same punishment that the falsely accused would have received.

SIMPLE SLANDER

There is no reason to conclude, however, that the ninth commandment was given for the courtroom alone. Although its language would be most at home in a courtroom, each word can be understood more broadly. The phrase translated "respond against" doesn't necessarily mean to give formal testimony in a courtroom. The same phrase is used of the young man who "testified against himself" concerning the death of Saul before David (2 Sam. 1:16)—he simply reported to David what had happened. Elsewhere, Samuel invites the Israelites to "testify against him" concerning whether he had defrauded or oppressed them during his tenure as judge (1 Sam. 12:3). And in Isaiah the Israelites' faces "testified" against them about their sin (Isa. 3:9). While the language probably derives from legal vernacular, it isn't necessarily confined to that setting.

The same can be said of the phrase "false testimony." These words can be as easily translated "a false account," a phrase that is not necessarily legalese. So the ninth commandment can be understood loosely to mean, "Don't go telling lies about your neighbor." Indeed, in the Old Testament, it often seems to be understood in this way. In Leviticus 19, where the Ten Commandments are paraphrased and expanded, verses 15–16 speak about fairness in the courts. These verses warn against perverting justice through dishonesty or partiality, as well as failing to testify when that testimony could spare someone's life. But the verses also warn, "Do not go about spreading slander among your people. The phrase "among your people" makes it clear that the ninth commandment isn't just for the courtroom—it also applies to everyday social interaction.

Throughout the Bible, we find many warnings against spreading slander. The prophets condemn the Israelites for spreading stories about one another (Jer. 9:4; Ezek. 22:9). In the Psalms, we read that only those who don't slander their neighbors and who do them no harm may stand on God's holy hill (Ps. 15:3). The psalmist himself often had problems with so-called friends spreading tales about him (Pss. 31:13; 38:20; 41:6; 50:20; etc.). God promises that he himself will put such slanderers to silence (Ps. 101:5). The book of Proverbs contains many warnings against slanderers: "Whoever spreads slander is a fool" (10:18); "A slanderer separates close friends" (16:28, author's translation; see also Prov. 11:13; 20:19). The "false witness" and the "man who stirs up dissension among brothers" are included among those things that the Lord hates (Prov. 6:19).

The ninth commandment specifically uses the word "false," but the preceding biblical examples do not. It's not often clear from the text whether the stories being spread are true or if they are known to be false. The New International Version (NIV) translators have tried to distinguish between the two by calling false reports "slander" and true reports "gossip." But in fact, the same Hebrew word is used in either case. The NIV translators based their different translations on context. The translators felt that some verses referred to false reports, while others referred to spreading the "dirt" about someone.

In the broader biblical perspective, untruth isn't the principal issue. The main concern is malicious intent. Suppose Bill tells Mary, "Mary, I know you and Tom are supposed to be best friends, so it hurts me to have to say this, but I heard Tom tell Steve that you can't be trusted." In the biblical perspective, it doesn't matter if Tom actually said it or not. If Bill is trying to undermine Tom and Mary's friendship with no good motive for doing so, he falls into the category of someone who is "among the people" as a slanderer.

In the New Testament, we find similar condemnation of the tale-bearer. In Matthew 15:19, Jesus clearly associates slander with breaking the ninth commandment. The verse reads, "For out of the heart come evil thoughts, murder, adultery, sexual immorality, theft, false testimony, slander." It's no accident that these sins follow the same order as the last of the Ten Commandments. First, Jesus mentions the crime addressed in the sixth commandment, which is the prohibition on murder. Then, the crime prohibited in the seventh commandment, expanded (as has been discussed) to include a broader understanding of adultery. Next, he mentions the crime of theft, prohibited in the eighth commandment. Then comes the prohibition in the ninth commandment, bearing false testimony. This commandment, too, Jesus expands. He includes not only the narrow, legal understanding of the commandment, but also the broader idea of slander. The Greek word in the text, *blasphemia* (from which comes our word "blasphemy"), usually means spreading a false report. But again, it is evident that Jesus' concern with slander isn't that the information is a lie, but that it's designed to do harm.

In the Epistles, also, Christians are warned against engaging in slander (1 Cor. 5:11; Eph. 4:31; 1 Tim. 5:14; Titus 2:3; James 4:11; 1 Peter 2:1). In addition to the word *blasphemia,* several other Greek words for slander are used in the New Testament. One intriguing word that Paul uses for a slanderer is *diabolos*—a word that also denotes the Devil. Just as the Devil's job is to bring accusations against the people of God (Job 1:9; Rev. 12:10), so the slanderer goes about making accusations and undermining the reputation of others. Another word used to describe this behavior, *psithyristēs,* comes from a verb meaning "to whisper," emphasizing the cowardice of rumor-mongering. Another word, *katalaleo,* simply means to speak against another person. None of these words necessarily implies that the rumors are false. The main concern of the New Testament writers is that Christians should say nothing designed to cause dissension and hurt feelings in the body of Christ: "For I am afraid that when I come I may not find you as I want you to be, and you may not find me as you want me to be. I fear that there may be quarreling, jealousy, outbursts of anger, factions, slander, gossip, arrogance and disorder" (2 Cor. 12:20).

Although the wording of the ninth commandment suggests that it is addressing the crime of false testimony in a courtroom, its implications go well beyond such a formal venue. The principle behind the commandment is that we must not injure our neighbors with the words that we speak about them—whether those words are true or false. We see this principle stressed repeatedly throughout the Bible, in the Law, through the Prophets, in the poetic and wisdom texts, and throughout the New Testament. So "false witness" isn't as crucial a phrase to this commandment as the words "against your neighbor."

WHAT ABOUT LYING?

The principle of the ninth commandment might be surprising to those who have always thought of it as saying, "Thou shalt not lie." That's often the way the ninth commandment is presented to children in Sunday school. Even many modern "adult" treatments have stressed the matter of lying. When we look at the commandment as a simple prohibition on lying, we can find ourselves floundering in a morass of sticky ethical questions. I remember the moral dilemma that I posed to my Sunday school teacher: "What if an evil madman is chasing a girl, and she hides in your house, and the madman asks you if she's there? Don't you have to tell him the truth?" My Sunday school teacher tried to think of some clever way to tell the truth and still not reveal that the girl was hiding in the house. Some would argue that I should say nothing at all—anything but tell a lie, because a lie would be a violation of the ninth commandment.

It should by now be clear, however, that the ninth commandment has little, if anything, to say about whether we should tell a lie to protect someone hiding in our basement. Nor does it address whether you should tell your wife that she's still as beautiful as when she was twenty. It's not even talking about whether you should report the proper income to the IRS. The topic in the ninth commandment is character assassination, not truthfulness *per se*.

There is no doubt that the Bible takes a dim view of liars. The book of Proverbs calls lying lips an abomination to the Lord (Prov. 12:22), and the book of Revelation says that all liars will be cast into the Lake of Fire (21:8). It would take a broader study of the Bible as a whole, and a balanced understanding of biblical ethics, however, to determine what God has in mind by "lying" and whether he really condemns "white lies" and lies designed to protect the lives or feelings of other people. (Do people *always* have loving and righteous motives when they tell the truth? Are people always trying to hurt someone or gain benefit for themselves when they tell a lie?) The ninth commandment isn't addressing those kinds of lies—only lying that is intended specifically to hurt other people.

HOW RUMORS SPREAD

Most of us have played the game "Rumor" (it's also called "Gossip"). Someone starts a rather involved story and tells it to the next person in line, who passes it on as accurately as possible to the next person, and so forth. It's fun to hear how much the story has changed after it has circulated through a dozen or so people. But when a story is about you—and it is going around among your friends and neighbors—fun isn't exactly the word for it.

The game "Rumor" illustrates the way a story changes as it passes from person to person. But the game doesn't begin to do justice to the way a story gets changed, because in "Rumor" each person tells only one other person. In the real world, hard-core gossips tell rumors to anyone who will listen. Even bush-league gossips will usually tell a few souls. You might tell only a couple of close friends about some sensitive "information" you received—maybe so they can help you "pray about it." Before you know it, people are calling you on the phone to tell you the story that you'd only told a couple of trusted friends.

A television commercial advertised a super new shampoo. The ad begins with a lady shampooing her hair. She says, "I told two friends about Sudsy shampoo, and they told two friends, and so on, and so on, and so on . . ." Now let's suppose that on Monday the woman told her two friends about this great new product, and she doesn't say a word to anyone else. Each of these friends tells two of their friends on Tuesday. On Wednesday, each of these friends passes along the word to two of their friends. After two weeks, how many people do you think will have heard about Sudsy shampoo? The number is 31,967. In about twenty days, with each person telling just two people, the entire city of Chicago could share the news about Sudsy shampoo. That's how quickly a rumor can spread.

In real life, of course, rumors are rarely spread from one person to an entire town—unless, of course, the entire town is really interested in the story. In that case, it can spread in a lot less time than two weeks. If the story interests a lot of people, mass media can be used to spread the word. Newspapers and television are not required to verify the truth or falsehood of a story before they broadcast it, though they usually try to make certain their sources are reliable. The media are only required to state that the story is "alleged." The tabloid papers have repeatedly won lawsuits brought against them by slandered celebrities because the laws in the United States allow a great deal of latitude in regard to the "freedom of the press." "The right of the people to know" is often considered of greater importance in modern society—particularly in the United States—than the protection of privacy.

The media can make a profit by feeding our voyeuristic tendencies. It's not surprising that the tabloid gossip-sheet *The National Enquirer* claims to have the largest circulation of any paper in America. Nor is it a shock that the sleazy, voyeuristic "Jerry Springer Show" has managed to match the ratings of the queen of mainline talk TV, "The Oprah Winfrey Show." Americans greedily devour the most unseemly details about the lives of celebrities. Witness the public feeding frenzy surrounding President Clinton's extramarital affair with Monica Lewinski. Even the explicit, excruciatingly detailed report filed by Kenneth Starr, made available to the masses via bookstores and the Internet, seemed unable to sate the public's lust for the latest news on the affair.

Even Christian ministries and media can be overly eager to disseminate negative stories. Each day in my office I receive letters from ministries providing me with sleazy bits of news about Hollywood celebrities, political figures, or other ministries. The informants claim to be providing important information about the downfall of our society or passing along special "prayer requests." Sometimes these letters represent legitimate concerns, but more often, all they do is spread rumors. For decades, a false rumor spread through Christian circles that the Proctor and Gamble Corporation was allied with Satanism because of the moon on their logo. The rumor grew to include stories of Black Masses held in Proctor and Gamble headquarters and curses being placed on competitors. TV preachers called for boycotts of the giant company. Proctor and Gamble was good-natured about the situation, but understandably upset. They invested a lot of money and energy into trying to put the false rumors to rest—

actually sending out letters to many churches and Christian organizations explaining that the organization was *not* Satanist.

BELIEVING THE WORST

It is amazing to think that such a flimsy story about the corporation would have spread so quickly and grown so big. But people have a perverse tendency to believe the worst about others. James Fenimore Cooper expressed well this human characteristic: "Everyone says it, and what everybody says must be true."

Several years ago, a young man charged the late Joseph Cardinal Bernardin, the Catholic cardinal for the Chicago area, with sexually assaulting him when he was a young boy. The young man told how a therapist had helped him to remember the incidents, and that those incidents had led to his later life as a promiscuous homosexual. The young man accused the cardinal of starting him on the path that led to his contracting AIDS. As the story made its way through the media, the young man talked with investigators and other therapists. Soon, it became clear that the events that he thought he remembered could not have happened. He was a victim of "false memory syndrome"—the therapist had used suggestion to create a memory of events that had never taken place. In this case, the story has a happy ending. Cardinal Bernardin's reputation suffered no lasting damage. The young man met with the cardinal, confessed his sins, and actually returned to the church. Many in the news media, slightly abased, admitted that they might not have handled the story the best way possible.

One clear lesson from this situation is that people are quick to accept even the most shocking stories. Cardinal Bernardin was well-loved and well-respected. No one had ever accused him of the least impropriety. Yet the accusations brought a storm of protesters and pickets to his home. They marched up and down the streets and shouted insults at the priest and the Catholic Church. A news reporter interviewed one of the protesters. He asked the young woman, "So you believe the story?" With pursed lips, she replied, "I have no reason not to believe it!" In her eyes, the cardinal was guilty until proven innocent. Unfortunately, hers is a typical attitude. The court of public opinion is often much crueler—and more unfair—than the court of law.

Thus, we need to be careful about what we say, because people can take it seriously. Perhaps one of the most dangerous phrases in our language is, "I don't know if this is true, so don't quote me, but. . . ."

THE DAMAGE OF A RUMOR

Shakespeare wrote well of "Slander, whose edge is sharper than the sword, whose tongue outvenoms all the worms of the Nile. . . ." When a story spreads and people believe it, the damage can be deadly. The book of Proverbs says a rumor can separate close friends. It can also destroy marriages. It can cost people their jobs and their reputations. My grandfather was, like me, a minister, and his work in one church was almost destroyed by a rumor-monger. Noticing that my grandparents frequently drove a lady friend to church meetings, a gossip-monger started a rumor that my grandfather was having an affair with the friend. When she later learned that it was my grandmother, not my grandfather, who usually chauffeured the lady around, she started a new rumor—that my grandmother and the family friend were lesbian lovers! There was no reason for anyone to pay these ludicrous stories the least attention. Yet, people did. My grandfather found his ministry constantly undermined at that church by slander and backbiting.

I could tell many more such stories, but the Jewish rabbis have a story that so well illustrates the damaging effects of a rumor. A man in a certain town became angry with his rabbi, so he made up some stories about the rabbi and told them to a number of people. Later, after the man had cooled off, he felt sorry for his sin. He went to the rabbi to ask forgiveness.

"It's not enough simply to ask for forgiveness," said the rabbi. "You must perform an act of penance to show how sorry you are for your sin. Go to your home and get a fine goose feather pillow. Cut the pillow open and remove the feathers. Lay one feather at the door of every home where you told your lies. Then return to me in a week to receive the rest of your penance."

The man gladly followed the instructions. He placed a goose feather at the door of each house where he'd spread rumors. Then a week later he returned to the rabbi.

"Rabbi, I've done as you told me. Now can I be forgiven?"

"Not yet," replied the rabbi. "You must complete the rest of your penance. Go and gather the feathers that you left at the doors, and put them back in the pillow."

The man was dumbfounded. "But rabbi! That's impossible," he said. "By now, the wind has spread the feathers all over town, and who knows where else! It would be impossible to gather them all up again!"

"Yes," answered the rabbi. "And now, do you understand what damage your rumors have done to me? They've been spread far and wide, and the damage can never be reversed."

Words have great power. With words, we can bless and heal, or we can curse and wound. The stories we tell in our idle hours can inflict great pain on others. They can also come back to haunt us. Jesus said that the time will come when we will be called to give account for every idle word we speak (Matt. 12:36). It's a solemn warning to bring our tongues under control, or be prepared to do a good deal of squirming on Judgment Day.

ABSENCE OF MALICE?

In libel cases, one of the most important issues is whether a person who printed or spoke untrue words about another did so with malicious intent. If a person spreads a story with the intent of hurting another, that person can be sued for libel. If there wasn't any malicious intent—if, for instance, a newspaper printed a negative story about someone but believed the story was true and significant—then the libel laws generally won't apply. The reporters might be guilty of irresponsible journalism, but not of libel.

Is the same criterion sufficient for judging the sinfulness of gossiping? Obviously, if people are spreading a rumor with the intention of deliberately hurting another person, they've committed a sin. But not every storyteller has injury as his or her intention. Some people feel morally compelled to tell about something they have seen or heard. There could be times when keeping silent would be sinful. If, for instance, you heard that a teacher in your child's school had a history of sexually abusing minors, you should tell someone. Yet you should still be very selective about whom you tell. It wouldn't be wise to spread a rumor like that to all the other parents in the school and start a panic. Instead, it would be far better to talk to the police or the school administrators, who could actually investigate the situation. If you reacted in this manner, you wouldn't be perpetuating a rumor. You wouldn't be engaging in slander. You'd be doing your part to defuse a potentially dangerous situation, or perhaps to save the reputation of an innocent victim of slander.

Sometimes when people spread rumors it has little to do with morality or malice. Rather, they may desire to build intimacy with their friends. Talking about others who aren't part of the clique builds a sense of closeness among the clique members. Other tale-bearers could be motivated by a desire to feel important, to look like someone who's "in the know." The motive could even be a morbid fascination with other people's pain. The Bible doesn't say that people who spread rumors for these reasons are necessarily evil. It simply says that they are foolish and not to be trusted (Prov. 10:18). A gossip is generally popular only with other gossips. No one wants to risk confiding in a gossip and becoming an item in the "Home-Town Tattler." Most people would do well to heed the proverb, "A gossip betrays a confidence; so avoid a man who talks too much" (Prov. 20:19).

Any number of reasons could explain why someone might want to go out among the people as a slanderer. Not all of the reasons involve a desire to cause injury, and so do not fall under the rule of the ninth commandment. But, the Bible certainly takes a dim view of all gossips and gossiping. Thus, Christians should make it a policy to follow their mothers' old rule: If you can't say something nice about someone, say nothing at all. Or, as the apostle Paul put it, "Do not let any unwholesome talk come out of your mouths, but only what is helpful for building others up" (Eph. 4:29).

TAMING THE WILD TONGUE

The ninth commandment seems quite specific in forbidding false testimony. False testimony is proscribed because of the undeserved injury that it can do. It's no great leap to infer that the principle behind this commandment includes any slanderous remarks, whether true (from the teller's point of view) or false. The most critical point is to restrain our tongues from words that are intended to hurt others. The apostle James writes that God wants us to bridle our tongues and bring them under control (see James 3:3-12). If we can master that feat, we probably have little to fear from our other bodily members. No doubt, the Bible says so much about slander and gossip because they are such a common problem. Almost every human body comes equipped with a tongue. And almost every tongue seems to come with a mind of its own.

Perhaps the first step in taming the tongue is mastery of the ears. If we won't listen to gossip, we're not likely to repeat it. It might not make you popular to say, "I'm sorry, but I really don't think I need to hear this." But it won't be long before you're excluded from the grapevine. Nothing throws a wet blanket on a gossip's fun like a good case of guilty conscience. So if your friends can't control their need to tell you gossip, they will just start avoiding you altogether.

Another step in curing the gossip habit is to fill your mind and your time with things that are better than the latest news about your neighbors. Charles Allen wrote in his book, *God's Psychiatry,* "Those of great minds discuss ideas, people of mediocre minds discuss events, and those of small minds discuss other people." As you get truly engaged in issues and ideas, discussing people can seem like a rather trivial endeavor. Read a book. Take a class. Give yourself something worthwhile to talk about, and meet people with whom you can talk about it.

You might also put your imagination to work. Imagine how you'd feel if the person you were gossiping about were to walk into the room at that very moment. If you can't say it in his or her presence, should you be saying it at all?

Finally, don't forget the most powerful resource of all: the power of prayer. It is through prayer that you can be "transformed by the renewing of your mind" (Rom. 12:2). There is nothing wrong with your tongue that a change of heart won't cure. If your heart is truly full of love and blessings, your mouth won't be full of slander and curses.

QUESTIONS FOR REFLECTION

1. Do you know anyone who has been injured by slander or false testimony? What is your opinion of the slanderer?
2. Did the Mosaic Law provide sufficient safeguards against false testimony? Do you think the ancient Israelite system was better or worse than our own?
3. How are slander and perjury similar? How are they different?
4. How do you distinguish between gossip and slander?
5. What do you think motivates most gossips? Is there such a thing as "innocent" gossip, or is all gossip wrong?

t w e l v e

A Contented Heart

You shall not covet your neighbor's house. You shall not covet your neighbor's wife, or his manservant or maidservant, his ox or donkey, or anything that belongs to your neighbor.
—Exodus 20:17

ACCORDING TO SOME SOCIAL thinkers and theologians, "sin" can only be understood in light of the commandment, "Love your neighbor as yourself." Any loving act is morally good; any act that hurts someone else is bad. An act that doesn't harm someone else can't really be wrong. We can't, they would say, judge anything that people do in the privacy of their own homes. As long as they aren't hurting anyone else, they can do anything they want. These people would claim, then, that doing recreational drugs in the privacy of one's own home isn't a sin. After all, no one is hurt, except maybe the person who is taking the drugs. Homosexuality can't be considered sinful, as long as it occurs between two consenting adults. Extramarital affairs aren't sinful, as long as no one gets hurt in the process. Indeed, under certain circumstances, extramarital sex could be an act of love and *good* by definition. Also, anything that happens within our own bodies—anything that has to do with our thoughts or attitudes—falls outside the definition of sin, since it has nothing to do with the way we love our fellow creatures.

The tenth commandment argues otherwise. Sin can't be boiled down to a simple formula of good or bad social interactions. Sin is a matter of failing to fulfill our obligations to God, a fact made abundantly clear throughout the Ten Commandments. The commandments address first our relationship with God. They then turn to behaviors that injure our neighbors. But the final commandment isn't about something we do to other people. The sin of covetousness—wanting what belongs to someone else—seems to injure no one but the sinner. As long, that is, as it remains in the mind. Covetousness can, however, lead us to injure others, as we'll discuss below. But, the tenth commandment itself deals only with what happens on the inside of an individual. And as we've seen so often, sin can be as much a matter of the heart as it is a matter of the body.

The tenth commandment offers the clearest evidence that the Ten Commandments were not designed to be a civil law code. No code of law would presuppose to tell you what to think. (Although Communism endeavored to *change* thinking, thought in itself was not addressed in its laws.) No police force would want to be responsible for enforcing such a law. No judge would consent to hear such a case. Even in the Bible, there's not a single example of anyone being tried or punished for covetousness alone. It is only when the "wanting" gives way to the "taking" that the community becomes involved and undertakes to punish the offender. Otherwise, covetousness remains an issue between the sinner and God, who alone can see the heart and mind.

COVETOUSNESS DEFINED

Often the interactions between little children are not pretty sights. As I write this, my own children are still quite young, and they haven't yet learned how to behave like civilized people. My son Vincent can be fully engrossed with a toy truck, but if my daughter Bethany toddles by with the blue ball, Vincent suddenly *needs* to be playing with the blue ball. The truck has lost all its charms. Or, if Bethany is eating her oatmeal, and Vincent gets a plate of eggs, Bethany suddenly gets an urge for eggs—*Vincent's* eggs.

Little children provide the most blatant examples of sinful coveting that we are likely to see. Coveting in itself, however, isn't always sinful. The Hebrew verb means simply to desire something deeply. But desire isn't always bad. In fact, the Bible has no quarrel with people who want something deeply, as long as they want the right things. Such desire can actually be a good thing. When the psalmist writes that his soul thirsts and pants for God, he's writing about a deep desire, even a *lust* for God's blessing (Ps. 63:1). Peter likewise tells us to long for the "sincere milk of the word" (1 Peter 2:2 KJV). Paul tells us that we should covet the best spiritual gifts, especially that we should prophesy (1 Cor. 12:31; 14:39). But "good desire" refers to not only spiritual matters. Paul writes about "earnestly desiring" to see the Roman Christians (Rom. 1:11). Could souls have been saved, churches established, or social injustice exposed, if someone hadn't earnestly desired to see the work done? So, it's not sinful to desire, or even to intensely desire. Desire becomes sin when the sinner covets something that belongs to someone else. Thus the Bible doesn't say simply "You shall not covet." It says, "You shall not covet your neighbor's house . . . or anything that belongs to your neighbor."

When you see a car in Mr. Jones's driveway, it is not necessarily coveting to say, "Wow, wouldn't I like one of those!" The danger is in saying, "What's a bum like Jones doing with a car like that? I want that car!" Yes, it's a juvenile reaction. If my daughter Bethany could articulate her own feelings, I'm sure they'd sound pretty similar: "Why has Vincent got eggs when I'm stuck eating this crummy oatmeal? I want those eggs!" And, of course, she tries to take Vincent's eggs. As adults, most of us have learned to control such impulses—we don't try to take Jones's car away from him. We might want his car, but we usually don't take any direct action against Mr. Jones.

Covetousness, then, involves not only desire. It involves jealousy, but a specific kind of jealousy. One kind of jealousy is for something that already belongs to you and you want to protect your rights to it. Several times in the Bible God describes himself as a jealous God, in regard to his exclusive relationship with his people (Exod. 20:5; Deut. 4:24; 5:9; Zech. 8:2). Sinful covetousness involves jealousy for something that is not yours and that you have no right to possess. That kind of jealousy is a focused greed, a narrowly defined appetite.

The last commandment illustrates well a principle that we've already discussed about each of the commandments. Sin is as much—or more—a state of the heart as it is an action of the body, and it starts when we turn away from God and others and place our own desires first. The actions of our bodies, the sins we commit with our members, are but the outward manifestation of the sickness in our souls.

COVETING AS A "GATEWAY SIN"

Coveting is often the first step toward flagrant sin. Few people steal without first wanting something that belongs to someone else. Few people commit adultery without first wanting to possess (or at least borrow) someone else's spouse. Paul warned Timothy that the love of money is a root of all kinds of evil (see 1 Tim. 6:10)—and that's especially true when it is someone else's money that we love. The apostle James eloquently describes how thinking in sin leads to acting in sin:

> When tempted, no one should say, "God is tempting me."
> For God cannot be tempted by evil, nor does he tempt anyone; but each one is tempted when, by his own evil desire, he is dragged away and enticed. Then, after desire has conceived, it gives birth to sin; and sin, when it is full-grown, gives birth to death. (James 1:13–15)

The story of Naboth in the book of 1 Kings illustrates this process. You may recall that Naboth owned a vineyard near King Ahab's palace. Ahab decided that the vineyard would make a nice royal vegetable garden. He tried to buy the property, but Naboth refused to sell. Ahab became depressed and sulked around the palace, catching the attention of his wife, Jezebel. "What's the matter, pumpkin?" she asked.

"Oh, it's that mean old Naboth. He won't sell me his vineyard!"

"Don't you worry about it," Jezebel answered. "I'll take care of Naboth."

Jezebel paid witnesses to claim they had heard Naboth curse the Lord. Naboth was convicted and executed, and Ahab took possession of the vineyard. The incident so enraged the Lord that the Lord destroyed Ahab's dynasty (1 Kings 21). In the case of Ahab, coveting led to false witness, and false witness led to murder. In the words of James, desire enticed him, dragged him away, and sin, full-grown, led to death.

The most famous example of the effects of coveting is that of King David, recorded in 2 Samuel 11-12. During the season when kings would go out for battle, David remained home, letting his officers and troops take care of the business of war for him. One evening David strolled on the roof of his palace. Down below, he saw a beautiful young woman bathing herself. David watched, and desire enticed him and dragged him away. The woman was Bathsheba, wife of Uriah the Hittite, one of David's military officers. Knowing that her husband was away, David sent for the woman, committed adultery with her, and sent her home again.

Soon word came to David from Bathsheba: "I'm pregnant." With Uriah away fighting David's battles, David knew that Bathsheba would face execution as an adulteress—and he might be implicated, as well. David acted quickly, recalling Uriah from the war on the pretense of getting a report regarding the battle. After receiving the report, David told Uriah to spend the night at his own house, expecting Uriah to enjoy the company of his wife. But Uriah didn't go home—he slept at the gate of the palace. When David heard that Uriah hadn't gone home, he was dumbfounded and demanded an explanation. Uriah answered nobly that it would be inappropriate for him to enjoy the comforts of home while his soldiers struggled on the battlefield. David was set back, but not yet defeated. He told Uriah to stay another day, again hoping Uriah would sleep with his wife. He served Uriah food and wine, getting him drunk, but still Uriah slept outside with the servants.

David felt he had no choice but to send Uriah back to the battle. But he sent with Uriah a sealed message for General Joab. Joab was instructed to put Uriah in the fiercest part of the battle, and then order the rest of his troops to fall back, leaving Uriah to fight alone. The deed was done, and Uriah was killed. David took the widow Bathsheba as his own wife, thinking he had covered his sin. But God had seen all and sent the prophet Nathan to pronounce a word of judgment on the house of David. The son born to Bathsheba died in infancy. David's own household was later torn with strife and bloodshed.

Coveting led to adultery. Adultery led to murder. And sin, when it was full-grown, led to death. The last commandment is often the first one broken on the way to more serious sins.

COVETING AND DISSATISFACTION

In most cases the effects of coveting aren't so extreme. Few of us go from simply wanting our neighbor's car to stealing it or murdering him to get it. Coveting, however, can have other destructive effects. First, it is impossible for us to have covetous spirits and still be content with our lives and possessions. Coveting necessarily leads to dissatisfaction, a lack of contentment with that which God has entrusted to us, and discontentment can have some dire effects on our spiritual lives.

Again, not all dissatisfaction is sinful, just like all coveting isn't sinful. The world is a very imperfect place, and surely not everything that occurs here is God's will. Second Peter 3:9 says that the Lord is "not willing that any should perish, but that all should come to repentance" (KJV). Since many perish every day, it's clear that God's will is not always done on earth as it is in heaven. God doesn't expect us to go about with a beatific smile perpetually plastered on our faces, praising the Lord for even the misfortunes that befall us and our loved ones. Christians are not called to a life of blissful ignorance, pretending that all is well with the world. Sometimes, it is only our dissatisfaction with circumstances that moves us to bring them more in line with God's revealed intention. Heaven forbid if all of God's people had been content to allow the slave trade to continue, or had tolerated the persecution of Jews in Nazi Germany. Heaven forbid that we be content to allow people to die in their sins rather than share with them the mercy and grace of Jesus Christ. Dissatisfaction can motivate us to challenge our world with the gospel and all its implications.

We should also be dissatisfied with the current condition of our spirits. As long as we live in the flesh, we should be pressing on to greater glory and higher holiness. We can't be satisfied with the present level of our piety or the current measure of our service to Christ's kingdom. We should always long for more of God's Spirit, for more of God's call on our lives, and we shouldn't be satisfied with anything less than everything God can give us. As we noted above, Paul actually counseled the Corinthians to *covet* the spiritual gifts that are most instrumental in building up the church and converting the unsaved (1 Cor. 14:1).

Dissatisfaction, then, can be a good thing if it motivates us to spiritual growth or greater acts of service. But dissatisfaction can also be a bad thing. Several times in the New Testament, we are encouraged to be content with what has been given to us. John the Baptist warned soldiers to be content with the pay that they received (Luke 3:14). Paul warns Timothy about the love of money and tells him that "godliness with contentment is great gain" (1 Tim. 6:6). People who want to get rich, he warns, fall into many temptations that lead to ruin (6:9). The author of the epistle to the Hebrews echoes these sentiments. He writes that we should be content with what we've been given, knowing that God will never leave us or forsake us (Heb. 13:5). Contentment with our possessions, then, is a godly goal. We can't be dissatisfied and content at the same time.

In the United States, however, dissatisfaction has grown to epidemic proportions. Our desire to acquire has made us the world's greatest gluttons. The United States contains only 6 percent of the world's population, yet we consume 30 percent of the world's resources. The most developed countries in the world represent about a fifth of the world's population, yet they consume over 70 percent of the world's resources. These statistics represent, in part, industrial use of oil, coal, and raw materials. But the numbers also represent the rampant consumerism of the average American and European citizen. Each of us owns many, many more things than does the average person in lesser-developed countries. The average American eats about 40 percent more than he or she needs to maintain life and health. The majority of us—following the example of the federal government—spend much more money than we earn. Almost 1.5 million people filed for bankruptcy in 1998, usually because their spending so outpaced their earnings.

The social and economic price tag of our desire to acquire is a high one. We work more hours than we should to keep up on the house and car payments. Many mothers feel compelled to return to the work force soon after giving birth in order to maintain the lifestyle to which they've grown accustomed. Preschool children are raised in day care centers by underpaid, undertrained, overstressed workers. School age children come home to empty houses and spend their hours relating not to parents, but to television sets, computer screens, video games, and radios. A recent survey discovered that the average American child between the ages of eight and eighteen spends nearly seven hours a day alone with some form of media. It also found that 65 percent of children over the age of eight have a television in their bedrooms. The parents are too busy paying for all those TVs and computers to actually spend time with their children. There can be little doubt that we are fostering a generation of kids that will be more comfortable with machines than they will be with other human beings.

While alone and watching those TV sets, children are bombarded with messages saying that they need to buy more things—the brand-name shoes, the new and improved video game. They're told that they can't be cool unless they wear expensive designer jeans. These messages impel kids to whine that they wouldn't be caught dead wearing the store brand, which impels parents to take on more debt or work more hours to be certain that Junior doesn't get a complex because he doesn't have as many brand-name *things* as the other children.

Television, the Internet, and other media also carry to these unsupervised children the violent and sex-laden images that ooze unfiltered and unexplained into children's rooms each night. I recently saw a program on public television about a 1997 syphilis outbreak in Atlanta. The outbreak wasn't among the prostitutes or the winos. It occurred in a rich suburb among high school students, and the condition affected hundreds of them. These children of privilege were bored and unsupervised. Without guidance or restraint, many engaged in sexual intercourse at the age of eleven or even earlier. The older kids practiced every conceivable permutation of group sex. Drug abuse and alcoholism were common even among the middle schoolers.

Through it all, the parents seemed utterly clueless. As the journalists interviewed families in one palatial home after another, the stories sounded like a broken record. The parents were so busy with extra hours at the office, business trips, and dinners with clients that they didn't have time for their own kids. They gave their children everything they could want, except time, attention, and values. Covetousness—the rampant desire of these families for things—destroyed their children.

It's not just our own children who suffer because of American consumerism. While we continue our pattern of conspicuous consumption, a child in the Third World dies of poverty related causes every twenty-four seconds. More than a third of the world's children suffer from malnutrition. The real tragedy is that the world produces more than enough food to feed every human being on this planet. We have plenty to go around. The problem is, it isn't going around. It's collecting in pockets of plenty. America, as well as many European countries, devour huge pieces of the pie, and they search constantly for another slice. Undoubtedly our society will soon reap the harvest of covetousness. The rest of the world already feels the pain.

THE SPIRITUAL EFFECTS OF DISSATISFACTION

The physical and societal effects of our cultural dissatisfaction are chilling. But dissatisfaction has spiritual effects as well. Dissatisfaction can lead to two very destructive frames of mind: thanklessness and bitterness. Thanklessness means that we can't appreciate the things that God has already given us. We might be happy driving a perfectly fine little Chevy until we see a coworker driving a beautiful new Cadillac. "Hmmm," we say, "that's one sharp automobile. Don't know how he can afford one on *his* salary." Then maybe we say, "I wish my wife would let me buy a new car. This little car hasn't got enough passing power. I could get killed trying to get around a semi on the highway! And the seats are uncomfortable, too. There's not enough legroom for a dachshund. I *hate* this car!" Coveting makes us unthankful for the gifts that God has given us, because we are admiring what he has granted to someone else (or perhaps what someone else might have acquired without God's help).

Thanklessness separates us from God, not by his choice—but by ours. We don't wound God's ego if we fail to thank him for his graciousness. But thanklessness can lead us to feel that God is cheating us and that he favors other people. We don't want to be close to someone whom we feel is cheating us. We may intentionally distance ourselves from God, deliberately avoiding prayer or worship. We might simply neglect our relationship with him, thinking that he doesn't really care about us anyway. If we had a thankful attitude for all that God *has* given to us, we would realize how deeply loved we really are. Instead, we can allow thanklessness to sabotage our prayer lives and worship experiences.

Bitterness goes beyond thanklessness. Thanklessness might be thought of as an absence of a certain attitude, but bitterness is the presence of an attitude—a *bad* attitude. It is an enduring resentment toward another person because of what they've got, or it is even resentment against God himself. In Acts 8:9-25, we read the story of Simon the sorcerer, who coveted the disciples' ability to convey the Holy Spirit through the laying on of hands. Simon desired to purchase the ability for himself. But Peter warned him to repent of his foolish plan, that his envy had filled him with bitterness (Acts 8:23). James, too, warns against allowing jealousy for the wisdom of others to make us bitter (James 3:13-14). In Romans 3:14, Paul associates bitterness with cursing others. The attitude of the heart may be expressed in words from the lips.

While thankfulness separates us from God, bitterness separates us from others—big time. Tragically, bitterness is a short step away from hatred. What begins with a simple desire can grow into resentment, and resentment can progress to hatred. The story of Joseph is a good example of this progression. Joseph's father, Jacob, played blatant favorites with Joseph, and his brothers couldn't help noticing— especially when Jacob presented Joseph with a coat of many colors. The brothers began to hate Joseph because they coveted the love that their father lavished on his young son (Gen. 37:4). Hatred, of course, puts us squarely into the hands of Satan: "Anyone who hates his brother is a murderer, and you know that no murderer has eternal life in him" (1 John 3:15).

Coveting, even if it doesn't cause us to steal—or commit adultery or murder—can have dire effects on our spiritual lives. We look fine on the outside, but inside, our hearts can be far from God and righteousness. Like the whitewashed sepulchres to which Jesus compared the Pharisees, we might look good to the world, but our hearts can be full of corruption and death (Matt. 23:27). While people may judge us by what they see on the outside, God will call us to account for the state of our hearts.

HOW NOT TO COVET

There is a way to avoid all this unpleasantness: we simply shouldn't covet in the first place. We should be content with what God has given to us and not want things that have been given to other people. One may ask, "Isn't that easier said than done? Is it really possible *not* to want things that other people have?" Coveting does, indeed, seem to be part of human nature. Nobody has to teach us how to covet, as we see it manifested in the youngest members of our species. In modern Western society, our biological tendency to covet is reinforced by a culture that encourages the desire to purchase the latest gizmo, to have more and better things, to pursue the Joneses with a vengeance. Many of us have been conditioned to acquire as many things as our neighbors have. We have an ingrained need to feel as well groomed and well accessorized as the next guy or gal. Can we ever *really* escape the sin of covetousness?

The answer must be a resounding "Yes!" Again and again in the New Testament, we are told that God doesn't want us to sin (e.g., John 8:11; Rom. 6:1-2; 1 John 3:6). And God doesn't command us to do the impossible. True, none of us should expect to be faultless while we live in this fallen world. Our lack of insight into our own natures can cause us to stumble into sin, not recognizing it until it's too late. At any time, we might be found unprepared for a given temptation—our adversary is certainly that clever. Even our own bodies can work against us. Uncontrollable surges of hormones open us up to lust or anger, vitamin deficiencies make us depressed and argumentative, eating disorders lead to gluttony.

We will never obtain sinless perfection while we remain in our earthly state.

But we can certainly minimize the hold of sin by practicing godly habits and discipline. In a previous chapter, we discussed how we should avoid situations that put us at risk of sinning. If we learn to avoid temptation, we will also avoid sin. We can apply the same principle to the issue of coveting. If, for example, your neighbor's car always incites you to covetousness, you should try to avoid your neighbor—or if he always parks in his driveway, you might even move to a different neighborhood.

Does that sound radical? Perhaps. But if a person is tempted to maintain an extravagant lifestyle in order to keep up with his or her upscale neighbors, that person might do well to move to an area with a lower standard of living so the desire to acquire won't be so intense. Remember the words of Jesus when talking about the sin of lust: "If your right eye causes you to sin, gouge it out and throw it away. It is better for you to lose one part of your body than for your whole body to be thrown into hell" (Matt. 5:29). The words are equally applicable to the sin of coveting. There is no fine house, no good neighborhood, no prestigious address that is worth the price of our eternal souls.

Another way to cultivate contentment is by spending time among people who have nothing. Someone once said, "I cried because I had no shoes, until I met a man who had no feet." The anonymous sage had an excellent insight. While living in the midst of plenty, our thoughts can be constantly drawn to the things that we don't have. Our neighbor takes vacations to Europe; why can't we? My brother has a new computer; why am I still typing on this old clunker? Contact with people who have much less than we have can give us a shocking dose of reality. How much stuff do we really need in order to be happy? Do we really need all the stuff we have? Perhaps a short-term mission trip overseas, or even some time spent working as a volunteer at a homeless shelter, could provide a renewed sense of just how blessed we really are.

We have an even more significant tool in our struggle against coveting. That tool is the power of the Holy Spirit. One of the main duties of the Holy Spirit is to enable us to overcome sin. The Spirit works in our hearts and on our sinful attitudes and desires, helping us to overcome them before they become manifest in sinful actions. When Paul writes about the fruit of the Spirit, he tells us that those who "keep in step with the Spirit" will not envy one another (Gal. 5:25–26). When our very attitudes are controlled by God's Spirit, coveting won't be a great problem. We'll be at peace with the possessions, the talents, and the lives that God has entrusted to us.

The next and last chapter will discuss in greater detail how the Holy Spirit can help us to fulfill the spirit of the Ten Commandments. It is indeed a comfort to know that we are not alone in our struggle against sin and our fallen natures. We have a powerful ally who is with us through all our temptations, ever quick and ready to come to our aid.

QUESTIONS FOR REFLECTION

1. Do you think that all sins, even sins in our thoughts, affect other people? Why or why not?
2. How do you distinguish between admiring something that belongs to someone else and coveting it?
3. How do society and the media foster our sense of dissatisfaction with our possessions?
4. Has coveting ever led you to do something you later regretted? What was the outcome of the situation? Did you think about the unrighteousness of coveting at the time?
5. Would you be willing to sell your home in order to avoid the temptation to covet? What would you consider a reasonable sacrifice for the sake of holiness?

t h i r t e e n

The Invisible Ally

Through Christ Jesus the law of the Spirit of life set me free from the law of sin and death.
—Romans 8:2

IN THE PRECEDING CHAPTERS, we've observed that the Ten Commandments were not designed to be slavishly obeyed according to the letter of the Law. Rather, each commandment epitomizes some principle designed to help us live out our covenant obligations to God. Jesus made many of these principles explicit in his teaching. We have had to infer others from a number of Scripture passages.

If you had hoped that living by the principle of the Law—rather than its letter—would provide breathing room and loopholes, you are probably disappointed. In truth, the principles hold us to a higher standard than the letter. The letter says, "Do not kill." The principle says, "Do not despise another human being, created in the image of God." The letter says, "Do not commit adultery." The principle says, "Do not allow anything to undermine your exclusive relationship with your spouse." The letter says, "Do not steal." The principle says, "Act as a good steward of what God has entrusted to you and to others." In each case, the principle is far more challenging than the letter of the Law.

When asked about the Law's regulations on marriage, Jesus presented a principle that many people found hard to swallow. "Yes, the

Law says you may divorce your wife. But that's not what God originally intended. God had planned for marriages to last for life. If you
divorce your wife—for any cause other than unfaithfulness—and re-
marry, you commit adultery." It was such a tough standard that the
disciples replied, "If that's the case, it's better never to marry at all"
(see Matt. 19:1-12). Jesus admitted that not everyone would be able
to accept the standard—only those to whom it had been granted.

So the Law presents an unanticipated dilemma: the principle holds
us to a standard that is even higher than the letter. It is almost
impossible to fulfill the letter of the Law. How, then, can we live by
principle? Can any Christian really expect to live out the principles
behind the Ten Commandments? Or do we simply strive for such a
standard, only to fall short and experience frustration and defeat
again and again?

WHY CAN'T I BE GOOD?

Every sincere Christian has experienced the difficulty of striving for
holiness. We become convicted that some habit or action is not pleasing
to God. We pray about it, cry about it, promise never to do it again. Yet
when the temptation arises, we sometimes find ourselves quickly surren-
dering to a sin that we thought we'd put behind us. We ask ourselves,
"Why can't I be good? Why can't I do what I know I should do?"

Some well-meaning teachers would excuse us from such self-
interrogation. "Don't worry about it, my friend. The apostle Paul
had the same problem. Read Romans 7. He struggled with sin the
same way that you and I do, and he never overcame it. You should
just learn to live with it."

And indeed, Romans 7 does speak of Paul's struggle with sin. He
begins in verse 14:

> We know that the law is spiritual; but I am unspiritual, sold as
> a slave to sin. I do not understand what I do. For what I want
> to do I do not do, but what I hate to do. . . . I know that
> nothing good lives in me, that is, in my sinful nature. For I
> have the desire to do what is good, but I cannot carry it out.

> For what I do is not the good I want to do; no, the evil I do
> not want to do—this I keep on doing. (vv. 14–19)

No doubt many of us can relate to these words. Some of us could
have written them ourselves. The great Reformers of the church, including Martin Luther and John Calvin, understood these words to
describe a Christian's constant battle with sin, our attempt to live
godly lives, but so often falling short. These words, however, were
not intended to describe the Christian. As the great Methodist evangelist E. Stanley Jones wrote, this description of life is "pre-Christian
and sub-Christian." A Christian is not to habitually do evil and fail to
do good. If that were the case, John would not have written, "No
one who lives in him keeps on sinning. No one who continues to sin
has either seen him or known him" (1 John 3:6). In the Romans
passage above, Paul describes his life as a law-abiding Jew, when he
was striving to be righteous by obeying a set of external precepts.

The clearest evidence that the Romans passage isn't meant to describe the Christian life is the phrase "sold as a slave to sin." In Romans 6:16–23, Paul uses this very phrase—that the Romans had been
slaves to sin—to describe life apart from Christ. Previously living apart
from Christ and his Spirit, the Romans were unable to live righteous
lives. The sinful nature, or the "flesh," as Paul likes to call it, compelled the Romans to commit acts of unrighteousness. But now, Paul
writes, "you have been set free from sin and have become slaves to
God" (6:22). Therefore, being God's slaves, we are obligated to present
our bodies for his service, not for the service of our sinful desires
(6:19). Simply put, Christians are not supposed to live sinful lifestyles.
The outcome of such lifestyles, Paul writes, is death (6:16, 23).

Paul continues this line of argument in Romans 7. After observing
how we Christians have been freed from the letter of the Law to serve
its spirit, Paul reflects on how the Law had failed to bring about
righteousness in his own life. The Law was good and useful, Paul
writes, and it made him know what sin was (7:7). But once he became
aware of the Law, he found himself all the more tempted to break it.
Using coveting as an example, Paul writes that when he knew the
commandment, the sinful nature then *produced* coveting in him. His

sinful nature struggled against the Law, and he found himself a slave to sin. You can understand Paul's point from your own experience. If I was told, "Don't eat those chocolate chip cookies I left in the cookie jar—they're for the Sunday school class," I'd probably start to feel an overwhelming craving for chocolate chip cookies. Without the commandment, I wouldn't have known that the cookies were forbidden. I might have eaten them, but not because of a sinful impulse. But now that I have the commandment, my sinful nature has been awakened to the temptation of chocolate chip cookies. The commandment gave opportunity for my sinful nature to produce unrighteousness.

Paul writes that he wasn't actually able to keep the Law, try as he might, because he was sold as a slave to sin (7:14). The Law is spiritual. It presents a standard of living that is fit for spiritual people. Apart from Jesus Christ, we are not spiritual but "flesh," living according to the dictates of our sinful natures. Obeying the Law would be contrary to our natures, just as it would be impossible for a fish to live on dry land. What a wretched state to live in, Paul laments. How could he ever find deliverance from this life of failure and frustration? At this point in his life, Paul could have summed up his struggle with "Why can't I be good?"

But there is a solution, Paul writes. There is an escape from this trap of sin and death. Though our physical bodies are dead to spiritual things, there is a Power that can make them alive, able to obey the principles of the Law. Heaven help the Christian whose life is stalled in Romans 7, and who never moves on to Romans 8! It is there that Paul expresses, in eloquent terms, the core of the gospel message: we need no longer be slaves to sin. Through the Spirit of Life, we can be free from the law of sin and death.

In Romans 8, Paul writes that the Spirit produces righteousness in us. The Law couldn't do it because the Law was hobbled by our flesh. The problem, however, is not with the Law. The principles of the Law provide wonderful standards for a godly life. The problem is in us. We are unable, on our own power, to make ourselves act righteously. Fortunately, we don't have to be righteous on our own power. We have an invisible ally in our struggle against the sinful nature. The Holy Spirit, who dwells in every believer, aids us in overcoming sin.

Paul writes that when we walk by the Spirit, the righteous requirements of the Law can be fulfilled in us (8:4).

In Romans 8, we are told that though sin makes us spiritually dead—
unable to obey God—the Holy Spirit makes us alive again. Through
his indwelling—the Spirit "takes up residence" within the believer—
our spirits are empowered to live righteous lives. Paul concludes his
argument with these words:

> Therefore, brothers, we have an obligation—but it is not to
> the sinful nature, to live according to it. For if you live accord-
> ing to the sinful nature, you will die; but if by the Spirit you
> put to death the misdeeds of the body, you will live, because
> those who are led by the Spirit of God are sons of God.
> (Rom. 8:12–14)

TWO MISTAKEN APPROACHES TO HOLINESS

It's amazing how little reference you find to the Holy Spirit in
books about Christian conduct. I recently browsed a bookstore and
found a couple of books about the how Christians should obey the
Ten Commandments, but neither book spoke about the work of the
Holy Spirit in producing obedience. The message of those studies
was, therefore, incomplete. They make people thirsty, but they don't
tell them how to find water.

One mistake that authors make is to put great emphasis on Christian discipline or willpower in overcoming sin, while neglecting to
consider the work of the Holy Spirit in the process. Some of the great
devotional literature of the Christian church is guilty of this mistake.
Christian mystics of the Middle Ages spoke of the *via negativa*—the
"negative path" to knowledge of God. These mystics lived ascetic
lives of self-denial and rigorous discipline. They lived in caves with the
barest of essentials. They dined on bread and water. They refused to
speak with another human being. By purging their lives of any sin or
distraction, they hoped to obtain God's favor and be rewarded by a
visitation from God, a sense of unity with the Divine.

The mystics essentially had things backward: our human attempts to live holy lives won't persuade God to empower us with the Holy Spirit; rather, the presence of the Spirit in our hearts inspires us to lives of holiness. We can't "purchase" God's Spirit by acts of self-denial, any more than Simon the sorcerer could purchase the Spirit with money (Acts 8:9–24). If the work of the Spirit could be purchased in such ways, it is no longer a gracious gift of God, but merely a reward for human effort.

Thomas à Kempis, the great Christian writer of the fourteenth to fifteenth century, wrote the challenging tome *The Imitation of Christ,* still beloved by many—and which rarely mentioned the ministry of the Holy Spirit. In 1729, William Law produced what was considered his greatest work, *A Serious Call to a Devout and Holy Life.* Its emphasis was discipline and striving for holiness. When John Wesley (founder of the Methodist movement) read the work, he wrote that it "convinced me more than ever of the impossibility of being half a Christian." It awakened in him a longing to be fully devoted to God. Unfortunately, Law's book didn't equip Wesley to live the life he was thirsting for. Although Wesley devoted hours each day to study, prayer, and self-discipline, he still found himself perpetually falling short of the holiness he craved. Discipline, devotion, and righteousness that is based on human willpower is ultimately frustrating and futile. More than that, as Wesley said with a little different meaning, it is ultimately impossible. We can't live by the principles of godliness when our lives are controlled by the sinful nature. Only the power of the Holy Spirit can enable us to fulfill God's commandments.

But we shouldn't expect the Holy Spirit to "zap" us into a state of perfection. In the mid-nineteenth century, a new teaching spread across the United States that emphasized the instantaneous purging of sin from the Christian. Called the "holiness movement," its teaching grew out of a particular (and I believe partially mistaken) understanding of John Wesley's teaching. Holiness preachers taught—and some still teach—that after we have been converted, we can receive a "second blessing" from the Holy Spirit. This second blessing, they claim, purges us from our sinful natures, the inborn tendency to sin that is ours as a result of the fall of Adam and Eve. They call this blessing "entire sanctification." Some teach that entire sanctification is not a gradual growth process, but a crisis that occurs in an instant of time. From that point onward, some maintain, we live a life without sin. True, those who hold this view allow for the possibility that we could still backslide and fall into sin, but they consider such cases to be the exception rather than the rule. Once Christians have laid claim to the experience of entire sanctification, they are expected to live sinless lives.

I have known few people who claim to have actually experienced entire sanctification in this manner. Most of those today who claim to believe the doctrine have softened it considerably: "It's something we hold up as the ideal"; "It's a crisis point in our religious experience, making it possible for us to grow into greater perfection." John Wesley, who taught something like the doctrine of entire sanctification, never claimed to have experienced sinlessness in his own life. Instead, he said it was important to aspire to perfection and even to expect to be made perfect in this life. And yet, all his anticipation seems never to have actually made him sinless. Indeed, he was frustrated by his own failures. When he honestly assessed his own spiritual condition, he knew he could not claim to be sinless.

Before Wesley's time, the great reformers Martin Luther and John Calvin were convinced that it is the lot of Christians to struggle with sin throughout their entire lives. They had no delusions about having overcome their sinful natures. If such great saints of God as these couldn't lay claim to being sinless, who can? I was once told by a minister that he hadn't sinned since his sanctification experience seventeen years earlier—but his wife, who overheard the remark, told me later, "Don't let him kid you like that!"

In fact, not a single passage in the entire Bible teaches that we will be instantaneously purged from our sinfulness through an infilling of the Holy Spirit. Indeed, the Scriptures speak often of being filled with the Holy Spirit, but rarely in connection with the idea of sinlessness. Rather, the infilling of the Spirit is usually associated with the supernatural ability to perform a divinely ordained task (e.g., Exod. 31:1-3; Judg. 14:5-6; 1 Sam. 11:6). In the New Testament, the infilling of the Spirit is often associated with the ability to proclaim the gospel effectively (Acts 1:8; 4:31). The Bible also tells us often that Christians should abstain from sin (e.g., Rom. 6:1-2; 1 John 2:1), but it never speaks of the eradication of our sinfulness. There is not a passage in the Bible that refers to an experience that takes us beyond the power of sin. If such an experience were truly to be the norm for Christians, the New Testament would give us explicit instructions on how to receive it. Also, more of the great saints through the history of the church would have claimed to have experienced such a blessing.

THE WORK OF THE SPIRIT

If the Holy Spirit does not eradicate our sinful natures, how *does* the Spirit help us to overcome sin? Let me list a few ways:

1. The Holy Spirit convicts us of sin so that we will feel compelled to seek God's grace and forgiveness (see John 16:8-11). Unless the Spirit makes us recognize our need for God's grace, we can't strike out on the pilgrim's road to salvation. This work of the Spirit is universal—whether someone is already a Christian, a Buddhist, or nothing at all, it is the Holy Spirit who makes the person aware of his or her sinfulness (John 1:4, 9). Of course, not everyone will respond to this spiritual prodding, and those who have not heard the gospel can only respond with the light that has been given to them.

2. He guides us into understanding the nature of the truth (John 16:13). The Holy Spirit makes the gospel intelligible to the human heart. The paradoxes and scandal of the gospel are incomprehensible to the natural man. When the crowds couldn't accept Jesus' teaching that we must "eat his flesh and drink his blood," Jesus told them that his words were spiritual not physical, and that is why his words were incomprehensible to the crowds (John 6:63). But through the Holy Spirit, our hearts can accept a truth too deep for our minds to comprehend. Paul informs us that no one can even say, "Jesus is Lord," except by the Holy Spirit (1 Cor. 12:3; see also 1 John 4:2-3).

3. When we turn to Christ, the Holy Spirit makes our spirits

"alive" to God, so that we can respond to his call of holiness (Rom. 8:9-10). This "new birth" or "regeneration" is our initiation into the Christian life. In John 3:5-8, Jesus expresses the same idea in different terms. "I tell you the truth, unless a man is born of water and the Spirit, he cannot enter the kingdom of God. Flesh gives birth to flesh, but the Spirit gives birth to spirit." Our first birth is a birth of the flesh. The second birth is birth by the Spirit, and with that birth the spiritual life and growth in holiness commences.

4. The Holy Spirit strengthens us so that we can be filled with God's love (Eph. 3:14-18). Through the Holy Spirit, God's love is instilled in our hearts. Through his love, we are enabled to fulfill the requirements of the Law. In several New Testament passages, we are told that love is the basis for the Law (Matt. 22:39-40; Mark 12:29-33; Rom. 13:8-10; Col. 3:14). John writes that anyone who lives in love lives in God (1 John 4:16). In Paul's great hymn to love, 1 Corinthians 13, we are shown how love helps us to reflect the character of God. So when the Holy Spirit dwells in us and fills us with God's love, the nature of God becomes more evident in us, and the sinful nature loses its foothold.

5. The Holy Spirit makes the Scriptures understandable to us and inspires us through them to be obedient to Christ (John 14:23-26). Jesus tells his disciples that the Holy Spirit will remind them of the words that Jesus has spoken, so that the disciples might keep his teachings properly. For us, the words of Jesus are collected in the New Testament Scriptures. The same Holy Spirit who inspired the Scriptures can give us understanding as we read the Scriptures and hear them preached, so that they convict our hearts concerning unrighteous conduct. The Spirit can also remind us of the Scriptures that are appropriate in different circumstances, so that we can better grasp the counsel of God in the face of temptations or ambiguous situations. It is important, then, that we devote ourselves, just as Paul encouraged Timothy (2 Tim. 3:15-17), to the study of the Scriptures.

6. The Holy Spirit leads us into righteousness (Gal. 5:18). He provides us with direction, instructing us in the way we should go. Jesus also spoke about this ministry of the Spirit. In John 16:13, he tells his disciples that when the Holy Spirit comes, he will lead the way into all truth. In this case, Jesus seems to be talking about the Spirit's role in forming our theology rather than forming our character, but the language and work are similar in both cases. The Spirit doesn't force us into a godly mold so that our nature is automatically conformed to the nature of God. Nor does the Spirit pull us toward righteousness as we kick and scream against his power. He *leads* us, just as a shepherd would lead his flock. It is a gentle process, but a firm one.

OUR RESPONSE TO THE SPIRIT

All these ministries of the Spirit are gracious gifts from God. We don't have to merit them. We don't do anything for them; we need only accept them. They are available to us, whether or not we have received a secondary "infilling" of the Spirit. But each Christian must take responsibility for how he or she *responds* to these spiritual ministries.

In Romans 8:14, Paul says that Christians are "led by the Spirit." That implies some movement on our part—if he is leading, then we must be following. Indeed, in Galatians 5:16, Paul writes that we must "walk by the Spirit" (NASB). The Greek word for "walk" literally means "to walk about," and refers to the way in which we conduct our daily affairs. Each step we take is to be guided by the Spirit's direction. We don't just call on him when we're in a tight spot, or wait until our evening prayer time to do battle with some temptation. If we allow him to guide each step, we won't be indulging the desires of our sinful nature. Later in the same chapter of Galatians, Paul writes that those who live by the Spirit must also "keep in step" with the Spirit (v. 25). The Greek word used for "keep in step" is a military term meaning to be in rank-and-file formation. You might well imagine Paul exhorting, "All right, soldiers, listen up! Fall in line with the directions that the Spirit is calling out to you!"

This is the true role of discipline in the Christian life. Discipline does not mean rigorously putting ourselves under a rule or ascribing to ascetic practices in order to mortify our flesh and break its will. Rather, discipline means listening for the voice of the Spirit and drawing on his power so that we can respond with obedience. The entire process of listening and responding in a godly way should be Holy Spirit-driven. He illuminates our sinfulness. He inspires our repentance. He shows us what is needed to make things right. And he gives us the power to do it.

I once read a fascinating tract by a woman who had become a Christian back in the late 60s. She was one of the "Jesus People." Until then, she had been living a life of self-indulgence, particularly in the area of sexuality. She'd had numerous lovers of both sexes. No one had told her that when she became a Christian, she was expected to give up her lascivious lifestyle. But as she matured in her Christian life, she felt the Spirit speaking to her about first one unholy practice, then another. She resisted at first but, over time, through prayer and Bible study she became convinced by the Spirit who dwelt within her that sexual promiscuity was sinful. Eventually she aspired to a life of sexual purity and holiness. No one had preached at her; she hadn't read any books on the proper Christian sexual conduct. It had been the work of the Spirit, from beginning to end.

That's how the work of the Holy Spirit is *supposed* to proceed in every area of our lives. The Spirit calls us to the state of holiness, and the Spirit empowers us to attain it. Our choice is either to cooperate with him and let him do his job, or to be willfully disobedient to the voice of God.

THE HOLY SPIRIT AND THE TEN COMMANDMENTS

How, then, should Christians view the Law, and especially the Ten Commandments? If we're simply to obey the inward direction of the Holy Spirit, don't external laws like the Ten Commandments become irrelevant? And hasn't reading this book been a waste of time?

The answer, of course, is no. Because the guidance of the Holy Spirit isn't limited to the inner voice that whispers in our ears from time to time. As I mentioned before, one of the main ways in which the Spirit speaks is through the pages of Holy Scripture. Through the Spirit, the words of the Bible are made alive for us. They cease being a mere external rule and become an internal motivating principle. When the Spirit speaks to us through the Bible, a voice inside us answers, "Yes—I know that's true!" Deep calls unto deep, writes the psalmist, and the deep voice of the Spirit resonates within the depths of our soul, calling us into a life of holiness and purity. In this way, Jeremiah's prophecy of the "coming days" is fulfilled in the life of the Christian: "I will put my law in their minds and write it on their hearts. . . . No longer will a man teach his neighbor, or a man his brother, saying 'Know the LORD,' because they will all know me, from the least of them to the greatest" (from Jer. 31:33b–34).

Through such Scriptures as the Ten Commandments and Jesus' comments on the Commandments, the Spirit can direct us along the way of holiness—the way of perfection. Our responsibility is simply to respond to his call and to walk where he directs us to go.

No doubt, that's sometimes easier said than done. Sometimes we'll have difficulty recognizing the voice of the Holy Spirit when other voices are drowning him out or when we've accumulated too much worldly wax in our ears. At other times, we might know perfectly well what God would have us do, yet still feel a strong urge to do something different. The Spirit can speak to us, but he can't always make us listen. He can give us strength to follow the Lord (Eph. 3:14–17), but he won't force us to do what's right. The responsibility ultimately rests with each of us. Prayer is a mighty weapon in our struggle against the sinful nature. The Lord Jesus told his disciples, "If you then, though you are evil, know how to give good gifts to your children, how much more will your Father in heaven give the Holy Spirit to those who ask him?" (Luke 11:13). God *wants* us to proceed to perfection. He *wants* us to be holy. And he has the power to help us get there—if we learn to draw on it, depend on it for each step we take, each breath we breathe.

The Ten Commandments, like all Scripture, are written to help us know God and to bear his holy image. In themselves, though, they have no magic transforming power. Pinning them up on our wall will not make us righteous. Slavish attempts at conforming to the letter of the Law won't do it either. But if we allow God to speak to us through them and seek his help in practicing the virtues they embody, we might find in them liberation from the frustrations of unrealized aspiration. That liberation will make it possible for us to attain our heart's most profound desire—true, biblical holiness.

Questions for Reflection

1. Were you surprised to find that the principles behind the Laws were even more stringent than the letter of the Laws? Why or why not?

2. Are there certain areas where you especially experience the struggle between the impulse to do good and the impulse to sin? Why do you think those areas are so difficult?

3. Have you ever prayed to be "zapped" perfect? What was the result of such prayer?

4. Have you ever felt the Holy Spirit telling you that something was right or wrong? Have there been times that the Holy Spirit might have spoken to you, but you didn't recognize his voice at the time?

5. When are you most likely to say no to the direction of the Holy Spirit? What can you do to minimize or even do away with such incidents?